BOOKS BY ARTHUR KROCK

THE EDITORIALS OF HENRY WATTERSON

IN THE NATION

MEMOIRS

THE CONSENT OF THE GOVERNED
AND OTHER DECEITS

MYSELF WHEN YOUNG

MYSELF WHEN YOUNG

MYSELF WHEN YOUNG
Growing Up in the 1890's
BY ARTHUR KROCK

Little, Brown and Company — Boston–Toronto

FIRST EDITION

T 03/73

The author is grateful for permission to quote from the following previously copyrighted works:

Max Gordon Presents by Max Gordon with Lewis Funke. Published by Bernard Geis Associates. Copyright © 1963 by Max Gordon and Lewis Funke. Reprinted by permission of the publisher.

"Derelict" by Young E. Allison from *The Best Loved Poems of the American People* edited by Hazel Felleman. Published by Doubleday & Company, Inc. Reprinted by permission of the publisher.

Library of Congress Cataloging in Publication Data

Krock, Arthur, 1886–
  Myself when young.

  I. Title.
PN4874.K73A3   070'.92'4 [B]   72-8830
ISBN 0-316-50441-6

*Published simultaneously in Canada
by Little, Brown & Company (Canada) Limited*

PRINTED IN THE UNITED STATES OF AMERICA

INTRODUCTION

THE PHRASEMAKER of the *Boston Centinel* who described the Administration of President Monroe as "the era of good feeling" had his eye only on the Western hemisphere, because never in the history of mankind has there been such a period in the world at large. The same can be said of the many "Golden Ages" which have been proclaimed; for, as Pascal wrote, though man's creative achievements advance from age to age, his malignancy remains the same.

Yet there have been localities in a span of history in which the conditions of living seem to have overbalanced the human bent for destruction and the day-to-day problems were minimal in comparison with the pleasure of existence. This was true of the region where one individual, myself, grew to young manhood.

The purpose of this book is to set forth in more detail than in a previous one (*Memoirs*, Funk & Wagnalls, 1968) what life was like in that region for a growing boy, and then for a young man learning his way in the field of metropolitan journalism. In retrospect, though as always the times were good and bad, it was an era to remember with a mixture of regret that it cannot be returned to and of recognition that the progress of social justice would be stifled by the reversion.

But though on the global scale the period 1887–1910 was marred by many wars — of which the British-Boer conflict in South Africa was the bloodiest — even these were localized: the pandemic military encounter of 1914–1918 had not been joined. And while the forces of nature inflicted great human disasters, such as the Johnstown, Pennsylvania, flood and the great tidal wave that razed Galveston, Texas, the attainments of science were of a measure and of a quality matched by no equal stretch of history, even though some of the blessings engendered new problems.

The first combustion-engine-vehicle, invented by Benz, was exhibited at the Paris Exposition of 1889. In 1892 Dr. Rudolf Diesel produced the internal combustion engine which bears his name. Two years later, via the kinetoscope, the era of moving objects on a screen was inaugurated, one of the steps which led to both sound and picture through the media of television.

Roentgen discovered the X ray. Marconi, in 1896,

patented wireless communication and made it operable in 1901 by sending a message from Cornwall to Newfoundland. Becquerel in Paris discovered the radioactive quality of uranium, and in 1898 the Curies turned pitchblende into polonium and radium. In 1900 Dr. Walter Reed completed the research which led to the prevention and cure of yellow fever. Henry Ford founded the Ford Motor Company. And in 1906 Captain Alfred Dreyfus was officially exonerated of charges of treachery by fellow officers who had hatched the anti-Semitic plot that had led to his long imprisonment on Devil's Island.

Most of these great advances entered the public domain before I reached my teens (1900), and they must have been talked about in the family and in the community. But I remember only the Dreyfus case, and this because at the age of ten (1897) I had laid my hands on and was devouring the forbidden fruit of Emile Zola's *Nana* until an uncle, discovering me in the act, snatched the book away. So that when Zola, in January 1898, published his celebrated attack (*J'Accuse*) on the perversion of French justice, my interest in the discussion that article provoked derived from the fact that Zola was the author.

I know a standard attitude of youth is that the whole American past is an "irrelevancy," that nothing of value is to be learned from it in addressing the problems of today. Yet the present can be the past's deformed offspring. And this one is rushing with such speed and in such volume that even the youth who are "with it" are swept along the faster because they have been deprived of the historical markings which would enable them to swim intelligently in this mad tide of time. And the inexplicable decree of creation is that when the future arrives it is no longer the future.

The antidote for the false philosophy that the past offers no lessons for the present action — a philosophy by which so many intellectuals have led youth into the badlands of anti-intellectualism — is, in my view, a return to inspection of the past itself. Some of this inspection may be provided by these recollections. Moreover, the thoughts, diversions and disciplines in rural and urban Kentucky in the times covered here, may lay some innocent balm on the spirits of those who bear the enormous burdens, and must live with the daily menaces, of this troubled world.

The members of my own profession who think they have invented what they call "New Journalism" may discover in these pages that it, in another dress, is an updated version of the personal journalism which long dominated the press of the United States. The idea that it is new to compose the report of an event by recording every known or rumored word and gesture uttered or made by the principals involved, the "profile" treatment, is at least as old as Plutarch and was perfected more than a hundred years ago, not by the *New Yorker*, but by Macaulay in his essay on Dr. Johnson.

And insofar as this book is otherwise concerned, the words of the old woman in "The Eve of St. Agnes" directly apply: "But let me laugh awhile, I've mickle time to grieve."

MYSELF WHEN YOUNG

CHAPTER ONE

H OW HAPPILY I REMEMBER: the noon whistle
that announced the L&N train had arrived
from Glasgow Junction on the main line of the railroad. The sound of hoofbeats and the jingle of harness as carriages neared the depot. The stir around
the Square as merchants, lawyers and mounted
countryfolk awaited the delivery and sorting of the
mail at the Post Office. The bustle around the soda
fountain in Mr. Raubold's confectionery. The tramp
of feet into "the" restaurant that marked the noonday lull in the town's commerce that the train whistle
had inaugurated.

For a few boys, of whom I usually was one, it was
a happy ritual to be at the depot when the noon train
rolled in. We could hear it coming as it crossed the
bridge over Beaver Creek a couple of miles away. It
was a matter of great pride to be recognized by the
red-bearded Mr. McConnell, whose surrey was the
taxi of those times, by Captain Crigler, the conductor
— his high estate made even more glamorous by his

blue, brass-buttoned serge suit, his gold-braided cap and the heavy watch chain that hung resplendent over his well-nurtured belly. But especially proud were the boys who got a personal greeting from Mr. Payne because *he* was the engineer, and by the use of shrewd flatteries it was possible to be invited to ride in the engine cab with him once in a while to and from the Junction. Somewhat less desirable — because this might involve helping feed the fuel into the engine — was to be on a personal footing with the fireman (alas, I have forgotten his form, his visage and his name!).

After all these amenities we would return to the Square, purveyors of whatever news of the outside world we had acquired at the depot, such as the arrival of a stranger, established as obviously a V.I.P. by the city magnificence of his clothes and boots. We were dusty from the walk on the unpaved road, but it was the dust of adventure.

Not less so than Tom Sawyer, several decades before us, did we teen-agers of the year of the turn of the century seek to put into practice the military exploits of Wilfred of Ivanhoe. Armed with wooden lances, mounted on wooden "horses," we constantly reenacted the tiltings at Ashby-de-la-Zouche. The goal was to stay aboard and tumble your opponent, and the ratio of success was such that every household in Glasgow was equipped with salves and liniments.

Our family had a special salve with the remarkable quality of rapidly curing small wounds and some of the skin disturbances which outdoor life in a hot and insect-breeding climate inflicted. This emollient my grandmother prepared from a variety of ingredients, including ham fat, which she never completely disclosed.

One of my uncles set up a production apparatus for the concoction under the name of "Grandma's Salve" and tried to find a market for it, assuring the inventor it would make us all rich. But, lacking the marketing and promotional skills, and the capital, with which my Princeton classmate Gerard B. Lambert put Listerine into millions of American households, he never made a go of the project. And the miraculously healing balm never attained more than local use and distribution.

I suppose my grandmother's recipe was a hand-down from a remote ancestor in Bavaria, where *her* grandfather, she told me, was burgomeister in a small town named Eisweiler, as nearly as I can spell it. It would be more romantic to attribute the formula to an ancestor of the Romany breed. But her fair hair and complexion, her straight nose, broad brow and other definitely Teutonic features gave no substance to this fancy.

John and Bob Lessenberry, being smaller and skinnier than I, were my favorite opponents; and as self-appointed manager of the jousts I paired with one or the other until protests obliged me to arrange for a fairer matching. As a regular enemy I then selected my best friend, Frank McQuown, and got my share of the tumbles as was right and proper. When we were not tilting — exchanging after each joust the roles of Ivanhoe and Sir Brian de Bois-Guilbert — we suddenly transmuted ourselves into the Six Hundred at Balaclava, galloped our wooden horses around the Square, to the annoyance and peril of citizens, pigs, dogs and such cats as ventured from their sanctuaries under the plank walks.

Our wooden horses were not, as might be supposed, the toy rockers which, in those days, were the first gifts on a boy's emergence from infancy. Ours consisted of broomsticks, each affixed with a straw-maned wooden horse's head that was splendidly caparisoned. And we made as much clatter as could be attained by the hard striking of wood ferules on wood sidewalks, a joy regularly terminated, however, by the town marshal.

CHAPTER TWO

GLASGOW WAS BUILT around the Court House Square, from which radiated broad streets expanding into "pikes" and smaller streets and lanes culminating in dead ends. In the center of the Square in my boyhood was the Court House (the fourth structure of its kind), a Georgian, white-columned, many-roomed building within a white wooden fence supplemented by hitching posts, and surrounded by a spacious lawn of bluegrass. The rest of the Square consisted of four blocks containing the business community — banks, shops, stores, offices, restaurants, and the Opera House in which itinerant stock companies performed such melodramas as *The Serpent and the Dove*, and individual and concert musicales were held.

The radial streets were lined with large, comfortable houses, set amid trees in broad grounds, as far as the town boundaries extended. Behind these estates was the modest housing occupied by citizens of lesser income, and ultimately the make-do dwellings of the poor, in various states of upkeep.

But a separate section, known as the Kingdom, was occupied by the Negro population. The houses were superior to many of those where the "poor whites" lived, and the yards and gardens more carefully tended. The churches especially — painted or whitewashed — were meticulously clean, airy and handcrafted with skills enhanced by religious devotion. Whatever Glasgow in those days had of what could be termed a slum, it was not the Kingdom.

The "pikes" that broadened from the streets enclosing the Court House led to the capitals of the adjoining counties of Warren, Allen, Cumberland, Adair, Metcalfe, Monroe, Hart and Green. My family, after fire destroyed our house on the Square, lived successively on two of these pikes — one terminating at Scottsville, in Allen County, the other at Burkesville, in Cumberland County.

My memory of the first, a temporary family lodging known as the Ford Place, on the Scottsville Pike, is of a large, many-windowed frame structure with enveloping galleries (verandas), enclosed in a lawn of moderate size and backing on flower and vegetable gardens. It was there my grandfather, reading the *Courier-Journal* on the garden gallery, voiced to me his sorrow over the defeat of John L. Sullivan by James J. Corbett in 1892; there I helped stuff geese with corn to fatten them for Christmas dinner, and shared, though not with her calm, my grandmother's discovery of a rattlesnake in the pantry shelves.

But the house on the Burkesville Pike at the edge of town — this is as familiar to me in retrospect as my Washington apartment is now. It sat on Ritter Hill and thus was known as the Ritter Place, Judge Ritter's estate having sold it to my grandfather. A long, tree-filled lawn, enriched by flower gardens, extended from a musket-barrel front fence to and around the house, bisected by a driveway edged with maples which glowed like torches in the autumn. The construction was dark-red brick, faced by a white-columned portico and white shutters. From the rear doors the land extended past a pump, a lye hopper, a springhouse, an icehouse and a smoke-house, to the usual farm outbuildings (including a privy); thence to fields of cane and pea vines, a large melon-patch and stables and grazing meadows for horses and cattle. The back boundary was the Co-lumbia Pike, heading for the town of that name, seat of Adair County.

Except for the melon-patch in August, when the succulent crop was so plentiful that my playmates and I regularly got the bellyache trying to eat the surplus before it was fed to the certified swine of the animal kingdom, the rain barrel beside the house was the source of supreme bliss. Five feet high, wide-mouthed, wondrously crafted of bent wooden staves and brass hoops, the rain barrel offered a wealth of delights. When it was drought-empty, a four-and-a-half-foot boy could climb its sides and holler into it, making a glorious booming sound. When the water level in the barrel was sufficiently high, the women and girls of the family would dip out nature's elixir for washing hair (I am told on the best authority that no pharmaceutical compound is comparable).

Sometimes, a sense of deep Victorian guilt highly visible on her face, a family female would dip out enough rainwater for the lascivious luxury of a bath. But discovery evoked such a protest that the depredation was not soon repeated.

The front door of the residence opened upon a wide hall, reaching from the front to the back door, with a "parlor," dining room, kitchen and pantry on the right, also an office-study, and a huge living room on the left where most of the family life was conducted around a vast fireplace. The two upstairs floors were complexes of the many bedrooms required by so large a family. But our only bathroom, whose sole furniture was a very large porcelain tub on bronze lion claws, was a large closet off the kitchen and pantry to which the hot water was brought by hand.

So far as we boys were concerned, its daily use was minimal — the pitchers and washbasins in our bedrooms sufficing for the light toilet which was customary, especially in summer, among barefoot boys. I describe this toilet as "light" because, as I distinctly remember, my own consisted of washing my face and feet, slipping into a pair of pants with cross-braces, and, thus accoutered, climbing out of my window onto the tin eaves above the front portico and sliding down a column to land on a sward fresh with morning dew.

In addition to the fireplace, common to nearly all the rooms, the living room was further heated by a Franklin stove when the weather was inclement. There my grandfather had a special chair, so had my grandmother; and at nightfall the room was lighted by many oil lamps with green shades, making it a most agreeable place to converse, read, pretend to study, and engage surreptitiously in horseplay until commanded to leave off. One of the earliest telephones in the county was screwed onto the hall wall just outside. And among my vivid memories is that, when a lightning storm was in progress, a ball of fire would often emit from the instrument and skitter to harmless self-extinction at the end of the hall.

The "parlor," used only for important company, had a fireplace with silver-framed mirrors above the marble mantel; and, for furniture, chairs and sofas upholstered in horsehair that were more pleasant to slide down than sit on, a high-napped carpet and an upright piano. Small fry were forbidden to enter this palatial apartment save by invitation, but ways were found to disobey this injunction with impunity unless found out.

The last time I was in Glasgow, in the Nineteen Fifties, this house was the headquarters of the Barren County Board of Education, and I had difficulty in finding my way about, even to my little room over the portico. But, of all the memories crowding upon me, one, so given to vagary is the human mind, was outstanding: my uncle Edward, years my senior, dancing about the stove in the living room in his nightgown and chanting a kind of rune of his own devising:

> "Bo-shee, bo-shee, bo-shee hah —
> Ouch! I burned my bo-shee bah!"
> (For "bo-shee" read "behind.")

CHAPTER THREE

THE NEW SOUTH in my boyhood had not even
begun to supplant the Old South either eco-
nomically or socially. Hence opportunity to better
oneself steadily drew off the young white adults,
male and female, to cities near and far. By the time
I went to Washington, in 1910, as the correspondent
of the *Louisville Times*, three of my uncles had
sought their fortunes in the Far Northwest; three in
Louisville; one in Chicago, to which my parents had
long since repaired; one in New Orleans and one in
Baltimore.

But in my early years most of the family still lived
together in a house large enough to accommodate it.
We were more than a dozen at table; and as for such
staple articles as basic clothing, grains, canned
goods, etc., my grandfather ordered them in large
consignments. "By the carload," I used to boast to
my playmates, but this was an exaggeration.

This large personnel exemplified the family pat-
tern of the time — as an example, my grandfather

sired fifteen children. Of these, six were borne by his first wife, Marinda Nevil Turner, in Metcalfe County (three of whom died in infancy), and nine by my grandmother.

Marinda Turner's surviving children were named Cornelia Belle, Victoria Regina and Frederick — reflecting on my grandfather's part both a sense of his German origins and a devotion (incomprehensible to me) to the lackluster House of Hanover which gave Britain its monarchs after Queen Anne. This same tendency appeared, with two exceptions, in the naming of my mother, Caroline, and her brothers.

Frederick, the eldest of the brood, had married the town beauty, Mary Dickey, before I was born, and he lived across the pike. He was a large, bland man, educated at the Naval Academy and Vanderbilt, and it was he who directed my reading to the English and French literary masters of the eighteenth and nineteenth centuries. My mother's two half-sisters were also married and left the paternal rooftree. Victoria Regina lived with her growing family in another part of town. Cornelia Belle had become mentally deranged, the result of an accident which lost her the sight of an eye, and was a patient at an institution.

But her fate had not affected a congenital trait of plain speaking, as witness the following colloquy one day, when her sister Victoria Regina was visiting my childless Aunt Belle:

"Vic, how many children have you?"

"Six."

"You slut!"

The street accident which cost Aunt Belle her eye was a consequence of one of the episodes of violence that occurred when some of the citizens had imbibed too much bourbon or moonshine whiskey, a frequent event of Saturday night in those times. At that period the family was living on the Court House Square; and in front of the dwelling was a stile where guests could disembark and hitch their horses. My aunt was sitting on the stile, awaiting the arrival of a beau, when a fight broke out in the roadway among some drunks.

They fell to rock-throwing, and one errant missile struck her on the temple, the expense being the loss of her right eye. An unhappy marriage with a Portuguese nobleman — at least he said he was and in proof claimed the proud name of d'Acosta — aggravated the damage to the delicate structures of the cranium. Her husband vanished into the distances whence he came, and her condition deteriorated to the point where only an institution could provide proper care.

The house on the Square lives vaguely in my

memory, for I was less than five years old when it burned down. I recall that it was spacious; I remember the white-trimmed Georgian brick facade and, when I resummon its aspects from the long, long past, several others are especially clear.

One was the parlor (living room) in which my grandfather sat of evenings reading his newspaper under the light of one of the green-shaded oil lamps — a light I still think superior to any of the sophisticated devices which have supplanted it. Another particularly clear remembrance is of the expansive flower garden which, under my grandmother's green thumb, became a thing of fame and wondrous beauty, with box-edged alleys, a lily pond and a small grotto. Once her Maréchal Neal rosebushes bore more than seven hundred blooms at the same time.

In evoking the lamplit parlor I remember an evening when I, having equipped myself with a pair of small shears, sitting as usual at my grandfather's feet and becoming entranced with the white vertical stripes of his trousers which alternated with black ones, carefully fringed the bottoms up to perhaps six inches. With such quiet devotion did I perform this act that no one noticed until the fell deed was done. I forget what the punishment was; at any rate, I did not repeat the sacrilege.

Such recollection as I have of the house on the

Square has persisted for two final reasons. Next to it was the Glasgow Hotel, and when I was about four years old there was an oil strike a few miles from town and the hotel was crowded with drillers, prospectors and other operatives of the field. Though limited by family ukase to short visits among these fascinating strangers, I stretched my permission. Having announced that I knew all the latest songs, I found myself their favorite guest; and, encouragement forthcoming, sang them. "Little Annie Rooney," "Sweet Rosie O'Grady," "A Bicycle Built for Two," "After The Ball" and "My Coal Black Lady" were very popular items in my repertoire.

The oilmen, being then as now generous in their habits, took up a collection for me after the first performance, repeated it regularly thereafter (I not at all unwilling) and it was not long before I had secreted a hoard of about three hundred dollars. Dark was the day when my grandmother, discovering conduct she considered no better than that of a professional beggar, ordered me to return the money. But since there was neither means nor disposition among the oilmen to calculate what amount belonged to whom, I was commanded to give the money to a fund for indigent citizens. Which — I am sure with resentment — I did.

Deceit and stupidity on my own part were responsible for my grandmother's discovery that I had a secret hoard. The deceit was attributable to the fact that, though I had persuaded myself to the contrary, I knew when I took the oilmen's money I was violating her stern rule against the acceptance of gifts of value from "strangers." The stupidity consisted of my choice of a hiding place for the money: the roots of some rosebushes in my grandmother's garden. Since she was a most diligent gardener, ordinary juvenile intelligence would have counseled me to conceal the money anywhere but among her roses. At any rate, the incident ended my criminal career insofar as I can recall the events of my childhood.

The final reason for my remembrances of this house was supplied by my eldest uncle, Fred. We had been safely evacuated at the outbreak of the fire which eventually destroyed the house, but, at the height of the blaze, he rushed back into the building. Horrified, the watchers speculated on what could explain this act of apparent heroism. Was there a missing brat? No, the count of small fry was complete. Had he, realizing that his Annapolis uniform, or sword, or dirk, or some priceless jewel remained on the premises, decided to risk his life for its salvage?

The solution of the mystery was not long in coming. Fred emerged in a few seconds, slightly singed as to hair and bearing a book in about the same condition. Later I learned the book's title, but not until very much later did I understand why he prized it so. The book (illustrated) was *Fanny Hill*.

Chapter Four

My GRANDFATHER, tall, slender, bearded, ruled the "roast" with a gentle hand, but, when he laid down the law, obedience — even for this child spoiled by most of his elders — was expected and promptly fulfilled. His wife invariably called him "Mr. Morris," and to him she was "Henrietta" — sometimes just "Ma." He had made his way up the Mississippi to Kentucky from his father's house in New Orleans with a pack on his back and a small amount of silver in his pocket to become the leading merchant and unofficial banker in Glasgow after brief storekeeping in Hart County (at Three Springs) and in Metcalfe County (at Edmonton). At Edmonton he had married Marinda Nevil Turner, and, after her early death, had moved to Glasgow.

In resisting an attack during the War Between the States on the town by Quantrell's infamous guerrillas, who preyed on both Confederate and Union citizens, my grandfather had developed asthma from exposure in the canebrakes, also a minor gunshot wound which troubled him the rest of his life. Eventually he died of the combination, so asthmatic that he passed his last months sitting upright in an invalid chair, his long-ago-wounded foot corrupted by gangrene beyond the medical skill of those times to dispel.

But until his invalidism he was one of the most active, as well as prosperous, members of the community: chairman of the Fiscal Court, and thereby invested with the lifetime title of "Squire"; proprietor of the largest and most modern and diversified store in the area; owner of the buildings on the Square with "The Morris Block" carved on their lintels; and benefactor to the poor, particularly Negroes, with non-interest-bearing loans and donations.

He came of largely Jewish stock in rural Prussia and Alsace-Lorraine, and, had ritual and other formal worship in that faith been feasible in a community without a synagogue, would, I suppose, have practiced it. Since he regularly made business trips on horseback to Louisville, a hundred and ten miles distant, he may well have gone to church there. But his aunts were educated in the convent school of the ancient French cathedral of St. Trophime, at Arles. And no creed was impressed on me as a child, especially so because my father was a freethinker, and I drifted into agnosticism without exposure to ritual or other observances involving commitment to any denomination.

But the consequence was that I grew up without knowledge of one of the most ancient cultures. Of the races of man, only three — the Hebrews, the Brahmins of India and the Chinese — who were civilized in antiquity, projected their civilization into modern times. The present inhabitants of Egypt, Italy and Greece respectively do not descend from the people of the Pharaohs, the Roman-Etruscans and the Greeks. And, though the wandering tribes of Israel were, of course, more or less mongrelized through the ages in proportion to the use made of their women by contemptuous overlords, a Caucasian with even quarterings of Hebrew blood is a Jew by the world's definition. And by that definition a direct heir to one of the three cultures which have survived antiquity.

The definition is unique in that it identifies an ethnic group by creed, whether or not long forsaken. On the other hand, such populations as those of Spain and Sicily — conglomerate ethnic mixtures — are defined by nationality and geography.

Many stories were told of my grandfather in the community where he was greatly admired and respected, of which I remember one in particular. When the financial panic of 1873 struck, Barren County was not spared the intense pressure of creditors everywhere to salvage some of their loans, and, the word spreading that my grandfather was bankrupt, he had to take measures to prevent the report from becoming a reality. He gathered all the paper currency he could lay his hands on, made a large ball of it and went on horseback among his creditors throughout the county. To each he said, showing the roll, "I understand you are afraid you won't get your money back, so I can pay you now if you want me to." In every instance he was assured to the contrary and thus survived the crisis.

The roll, however, was more impressive by its size than by its content. For he had covered the ninety or more percent of it that was composed of one-dollar bills with bills of large denomination, and the sight of these dispelled the anxiety of the creditors. Eventually they, as well as any others to whom he ever became indebted, were repaid in full with the interest due.

My grandfather spoke with the soft accent of the South where his life was spent. Until his asthma developed into what is now termed emphysema, he was a pipe-smoker and chewed tobacco; drank three "toddies" of bourbon — with "a little sugar in the gourd" — each day on a fixed schedule; and sang country songs in the family circle. It was his unbroken rule never to discuss "business" at home, though he often brought business associates to the noonday meal — particularly those who in that time were called "drummers." On one such occasion, my grandmother told me years afterward, he embarrassed her as follows: When the main course was finished he asked her, "What are we having for change?" But that day, most unusually, she had none. I should explain that in Barren County "change" was the term for dessert. I never heard it called this anywhere else.

While my grandfather was the unquestioned head of the family, his wife was the equally unquestioned head of the household, a larger and even more demanding occupation. It involved feeding, bedding, disciplining, doctoring and administering the conduct and morals of a large brood that included the three surviving children of the six borne to my grandfather by his first wife, and the nine (eight sons and one daughter) which my grandmother bore. To these responsibilities she added the role of unofficial nursing assistant to our family doctor when some poor family in town or in the country had some emergency need for medical care, especially obstetrical.

In response to her sense of duty to humanity, she helped the doctor deliver so many babies, self-trained though she was, and regardless of the hour, that she was, in effect, godmother to a population. Yet the bunch of locker keys she carried at her waist was testimony to the extent of her detailed supervision of her large private domain.

My grandmother came of the same German-Jewish stock as her husband — her surname was Frank. But her features and coloring suggested a wider strain than his of the Teutonic. Also she was of the town and he of the country. She told me — for I was only seven when my grandfather died — that his forebears were farmers and cattlemen in Prussia and Alsace, while, as aforesaid, her grandfather was a burgomeister in Bavaria.

She had been beautiful when young and was still handsome in her fifties when I became aware that the lady who was rearing me was not my mother but my grandmother. Her brow was broad, her hair chestnut in color, her eyes light brown and lambent, her nose what is termed Roman, her figure slenderly rounded, her voice modulated. Harassed as she constantly was by eight active sons, I never heard her yell at them, but she could speak with cutting and effective firmness when the occasion warranted.

She was the source of my information on how she met my grandfather. She was living with relatives in Louisville, she said, and when she turned eighteen these relatives set upon matchmaking. Their candidate was a young widower, with three young children, who had a prospering store in Glasgow and a rising position in the community. He was described to her as attractive, kind and of the highest character. And, after this conditioning had gone on for some months, my grandfather appeared and began his courting.

I gathered that they fell quickly in love (a good thing, because obviously he had little time to spare before returning to his family and his business), were soon married, and set up housekeeping in Glasgow. However practical the considerations of both may have been at the beginning, this was a love match unmarred, insofar as anyone who knew them remembers, even by the hard words of minor quarrels that are common to marriage.

My reportorial instinct failed me in one particular where she was concerned, because, though I was in my early thirties when she died in her nineties, I never asked where she acquired the Latin tags which, with proverbs both sacred and profane, she used to fit arising situations. The possible explanation is that she had something of a European education in the classics. But she spoke in the accent and vernacular of our area, interspersed with ringing Anglo-Saxon epithets such as "slut" for certain females whom she suspected of "carrying on."

Apparently, as the rude country saying is, she "dropped" her nine offspring, for until she was very old, there was no physical slackness about her. And the only evidence she ever gave of wanting public appreciation of the help to others she gave so generously was her occasional reference to the fact that she had been introduced to William Jennings Bryan as "Glasgow's angel."

In her old age, she often searched vainly for spectacles that she had lodged above her own hairline, and, when one of her sons appeared, would remember his name only after she had gone through the process of a countdown from the eldest. She broke her hip in her late eighties but became ambulant again in a few months, to take to her bed permanently only when she lay dying something short of ninety-five.

CHAPTER FIVE

BEING THE FIRSTBORN of my grandfather's "second get," the only female of nine, my mother was treated as a precious object by her brothers: though her name was Caroline, to them she was known as "Dolly," inspired by the heroine of Dickens's *Barnaby Rudge*. She was a petite brunette; her face was not as pretty as it was pleasing; she was gifted with a grace of manner, a soft, melodious voice and a gentle spirit. However violent the quarrels among her brothers, they were on their good behavior in her presence. Her education was light, and in the subjects deemed appropriate for young ladies of the time — art, music, riding, poetry and Victorian fiction. But remarkably, in view of her mother's array of household talents — which extended to producing yarn and thread on a spinning wheel — she could embroider, but neither cook nor sew at the time of her marriage, and never well.

The eight brothers differed strongly in personality and tastes, but all were possessed of physical courage

— a quality both highly esteemed and essential in a Southern community where blood ran hot, and maybe still does.

Herman, the eldest, shared with his half-brother Frederick the best education of any: what now would be called prep school and then the university. Herman was tall, well built, good-looking, charming, and he made use of the latter quality with girls to a degree that would have earned him the description of "parlor snake" had that term yet been invented.

Herman was bred to the law at the University of Virginia, standing high in his class, and, until in middle age he removed to Louisville from Glasgow, was active in politics. He was very popular in the town, becoming its first city attorney, and his popularity was as great in the Negro as in the white community — some of it deriving from his earned reputation as a man whom it was physically dangerous to offend, some for his active concern for the welfare of the underprivileged. Had it not been for his passion for gambling at high stakes he might have risen to leadership in state politics and at the bar. But this passion eventually submerged his promising career in an overwhelming tide of debts he could not redeem.

To me this uncle was a dashing figure; also a kind and discriminating guide to reading which nourished my young mind, a source of perceptive kindness and understanding.

But the uncle whom I most desired to emulate was his immediate younger brother, Edward. Edward was equally beloved inside the family and in the community for the plenitude of gifts nature had bestowed on him. He was a delightful companion — good-natured, witty, humorous and warm; his blue eyes sparkled with merriment. Though shorter than his elder brother, he was sturdier, very proficient with his fists — but only when their use was thrust upon him — and an even better local politician (Democratic), witnessed by his election as Glasgow's first mayor after the town was incorporated.

He was also fortunate in his marriage. His wife, my Aunt Julia, was the center of my adoration from boyhood, and her beauty, charm and ready laughter abide with me. Her father, known as "Pappy" Smith, was a Confederate veteran whom the town never tired of hearing explain why he walked with a list: "I am full of Yankee bullets on my right side." When Aunt Julia, then a widow of many years, died in Seattle, to which my uncle had removed his family, she left me, in testimony to our loving relationship, a lace dress she made for me when I was one year old and which I wore until custom decreed that my time for kilts had arrived.

The third of my grandmother's sons, Julius, was

what would now be termed a "swinger." He was gay, witty, kind, tall, well muscled and born with the gift of laughter. He roved from one mercantile job to another, his life ending in New Orleans, from which city his father had started his pilgrimage to Kentucky. In the course of this itinerary he married, at La Grange, Kentucky, Elizabeth Ballard, one of the great beauties of her place and time.

Louis was slighter of stature than the run of his brothers, and one of those men whose gentleness of voice and mien leave people unprepared for the disclosure of a vein of iron when the necessity arises. In his capacity as chief of the town's volunteer fire department he regularly risked injury and death, for his concept of a leader was that he should lead — unlike Lord Melbourne's cynical comment, "I am their leader; I must follow them." He was an accomplished horseman, and, next to his wife and children, his love was lavished on the best of the thoroughbreds he trained, Lady Belle, on which he won blue ribbons at county fairs and quarter-mile tracks. His wife, born Emma Pedigo, of Huguenot ancestry, was so devout a communicant in the Baptist church that I was somewhat terrified of her godliness when I was small. But I learned in time to note and appreciate that, behind the beauty of a Spartan matron, were deep human compassion and a strong sense of humor.

Gus was made of the finest clay of them all. In a community where his father's integrity was cited to children as a model for emulation, Gus fully lived up to his ancestor in word and deed. His piercing blue eyes, under their heavy brows, did not, as Tennyson wrote of Wellington, "freeze with one rebuke all strong self-seekers trampling on the right"; for he was a withdrawn, private man who minded his own business. But if a wrong, committed or proposed, came within his orbit, he, too, could freeze the offender.

He also was endowed with the physical courage which ran through the family, plus a temper matched only by that of his younger brother Lee. In their youth this pair often came to blows, and in one of their encounters Lee threw a knife at his brother which left a lifetime scar. But, curiously, they were particularly devoted to each other, and it was Gus who pleaded with his father to end the strong discipline to which for a time Lee was subjected.

His wife, my Aunt Anne (Redding), ranked with my Aunt Julia in my affections throughout her life. She was an ash-blonde beauty of great grace and charm; her voice was as sweet as her nature. In my memory these two aunts live as objects of brightness and gaiety, and not only because they spoiled me rotten.

Lee's temperament was fiery, as described, but he

understood with rare perception the longings of a boy, and I was proud of his reputation as a champion hunter and fisherman. He was shorter and sturdier of build than his immediate elder, but when his nostrils flared, as they did in anger, I would have described him as formidable if I had known the word. And he had in good measure the wit, merriment and compassion which were the characteristics of his brood.

Because I was nearer of age to Joe, I knew him on a more intimate level than his older brothers. For some years we slept in the same bed; he guided me through some of the perplexities of adolescence; and, though I could not match his prowess in such athletic activities as football, bowling and the sports of the field, he encouraged me to do my best. When I was with my parents in Chicago, Joe lived several years with us. And after he migrated to Seattle, and finally Vancouver, we maintained a frequent correspondence. As I think of him, I find that magnanimity, gentleness, and unusual physical strength are the impressions I most clearly retain.

Max, the youngest of my uncles and nearest to me in age, was the gayest, though his physical courage was put to the test more often than that of any of his brothers. This was because the Semitic strain in his ancestry seemed to have concentrated by implanting on him its most definitive feature. His nose, beaked like an eagle's, curved like a scimitar, was an invitation to taunts which he dealt with as militantly as did Cyrano. The result was that in his boyhood he bore many scars of battle, but eventually none of his contemporaries was more respected, a status to which a lethal skill in boxing contributed.

Max was the pitcher on the Glasgow baseball team and a crap-shooter more skilled and daring even than the Negro boys (who were supposed to be endowed with something akin to genius at the hazard). He also was an imaginative teller of tales — a combination which impelled me to follow him around as my dog, Princess, followed me. Of his tales I principally recall one which in my childhood I firmly believed to be true, although snow and ice were rare in our climate. Max's idol was his much older brother Edward, who, he informed me, had skated on South Fork into Beaver Creek, then into the Big Barren River, then into the Green, the Ohio, and the Mississippi and so on to New Orleans.

The thoughts of youth are long, long thoughts, wrote Mr. Longfellow, and mine dutifully followed Uncle Ed on skates to New Orleans, which may be a record for what the poet had in mind. I felt sadly let down when I realized that the tale was only a product of my youngest uncle's imagination.

When Max was the pitcher of the Glasgow baseball team I remember one game in particular because of a conversation that followed between him and my father. Max had an assortment of fast balls and curves that bewildered opposing batters, although, because of weakness at the bat and its pitcher's wildness, his team lost games it should have won. On the occasion I remember my father asked him how many batters he had struck out. "Twenty-seven," Max replied, and it was true. "But," said my father, "your team lost, didn't it? How could that be?" Baseball experts can readily explain what would appear to be an impossibility: those on the rival team who didn't strike out got on base through walks; advanced around the diamond on wild pitches and Glasgow's errors; and Glasgow could not retaliate due to its feebleness with what sportswriters used to term "the willow."

Among my many first cousins my favorite companions were three—Frank, Charles Wendell and William Redding Morris. But in strutting my role as their senior, and one who had the cachet of interim spans of city life in the metropolis of the Mississippi Basin, Chicago, I was something of a petty tyrant, usually a benevolent one, though because Frank was held up to me as the foremost example of a "good boy" I sometimes subjected him to light tortures.

Both Frank and Charlie had sweet dispositions with which mine was constantly being unfavorably compared by the elders. I spent more time with Charlie because he had a turn of mind which reveled in my romantic reconstructions of history and the spoutings from the poets with which I favored him. So the lower angels of my nature, if any angels abide there, were not aroused by this cousin, and in lordly fashion I permitted him to follow me around.

William Redding Morris was ten years younger than I and a boy of daring. The result was that the tables were turned where this cousin and I were concerned. He jeered in company at my calf-loves in the very presence of the adored. And once this took the embarrassing form — in a winter remarkable in our area for contributing a considerable snowfall — of hurling snowballs when trailing me out walking with an older girl whom I was trying to impress with my sophistication.

In every way he was a spirited lad, and before he was twenty made national headlines by eloping with the granddaughter of our richest and otherwise most prominent citizen. His death in the first flush of his maturity put an abrupt end to his bright prospect of being the toast of the town.

My brood of first cousins had their own broods in the same relationship. Of these I best and most admiringly remember three — Michael and Porter Dickinson, brothers, and *their* cousin, Haiden Trigg Dickinson. Mike, who died early in Seattle, was a prospective professional baseball pitcher of the first rank. Porter is a newspaper mogul in Honolulu. Haiden Trigg served gallantly in the United States Navy in the First World War as a gunnery officer on the suicidal Queenstown patrol, and in the China seas. He was a legendary naval hero in the making when ill-health forced his retirement and brought him to an early grave.

The design of these boyhood reminiscences is to expose for later generations the lifestyle of the family and of a Southern community in the setting of the period. In pursuance of this design I have etched some of the principals and their customs in much greater detail. But with respect to my father I have little of relevance to add.

He was the eldest child of a cartographer who had migrated to New York City from the German segment of Silesia, the cockpit of the bloody wars between Austria and Prussia, where the name Krock occurs more frequently than elsewhere, sometimes with the variant of "Kroch" — as spelled by the famous bookstore proprietor (with whom my father discussed a possible but never-documented relationship). My paternal grandfather must also have had some connection with the Netherlands government because, according to his son, he drew the most detailed map of the islands of Java and Sumatra that existed in the first half of the nineteenth century.

Because my birth blinded my mother for the first six years of my life, and I accordingly was reared by her parents in Kentucky, and because my mother felt that my father's parents had not appreciated him, I knew little of my father's family, not even where my paternal grandmother was born or her maiden name. But when I became conscious that a person had two sets of grandparents I was told that this other set lived in Brooklyn, and my father with them until, having learned the trade of bookkeeping, he got a job in Pittsburgh and, after meeting my mother, removed to Kentucky. There he would have remained but for information that there was an eye surgeon in Chicago who had perfected an operation which could (and did) restore my mother's sight. The result was that, after my father had established himself there in a job of his trade, in time becoming an accountant on a small scale, my mother joined him in Chicago.

I continue to be mystified by the contrast between exact and vague recollections where my father and his family are concerned. But of the following I am certain:

My mother went on summer holiday (circa 1885) to Put-In Bay, Ohio, met my father, who was on vacation there from Pittsburgh; they became engaged and were soon thereafter married in Glasgow.

Born in 1859, and hence a child of the depression subsequent to the War Between the States, my father did not attend college, but, through wide and discriminating reading and the possession of a fine mind, could be classified as a self-educated man. He had a good writing style, vented through the channel of letters to the editor (the *Courier-Journal* principally); a photographic memory, particularly of the writings of Shakespeare and the British Romantic poets; a fiery temper (once he hurled out of doors a clock which had betrayed him by losing time during the night); very good looks when young — blue-black hair and eyes, a florid complexion and a graceful build; an intense and cynical interest in politics (I remember he once told me that James G. Blaine was "too intelligent to be President, even if he had cared more where his money came from"); and supported his wife and himself on a salary that never exceeded the subsistence level. But somehow this level included good food and whiskey, frequent journeys by streetcar to the racetracks for discreet two-dollar wagers, and an evening or two a month in billiard rooms (he was adept at the game). Also, he was a freethinker, which meant in those days an agnostic — a philosophy of the Creation that I share.

He lived for ten years after my mother's death, awaiting his own at seventy-nine with cheer and comfort, in San Diego, where I arranged pleasant accommodations (as I saw when I visited there) for him and an elderly female attendant.

In view of his interest in his distant origins, a curiosity which skipped me but my son has inherited, I wish my father could have been with me in Germany after the Second World War. For in Frankfurt a Catholic priest in Göppingen, Württemberg, after some correspondence, brought to me a tall *maedchen* of his flock who wanted to migrate to the United States and looked to me for help because our surnames were the same.

Her father, Walther Krock, had been a federal judge in Silesia from which he fled with his family from the advancing Poles. Her name was Adelgunde, and her blue eyes, golden braids and complexion of cream and roses were strikingly supplemental to the name. It would further have intrigued my father to know that Walther and Adelgunde were only two of more than a dozen Krocks, all from Silesia, who, having chanced on my name in the press, wrote to me during the Second World War from places as distant as a prison camp of German soldiers in England and a farm in South Dakota these Krocks had owned for generations. And my father, had he lived in Washington, most certainly would have made it a point to become acquainted with R. Temple Krock, who for years was a high civilian official in the Department of Defense. I never tried.

Probably because his own dreams of fame and achievement never materialized, he was impatient with the silly range of my own in middle boyhood. "You are one of those parlor generals," he was wont to say when I ventured some such nonsensical opinion as how Napoleon could have won at Waterloo. And he was quick to hurl this epithet at anyone (especially an academician) who, without practical experience in public affairs, offered cocksure solutions of the problems therein. That he was often guilty of the same arrogance simply demonstrates the truth, common to all sound philosophy and experience, that the ways of man are the most inconsistent among the animals.

It was to his own positiveness of what was right and what was wrong that I owe my given name: none in the family, before or since, has borne it. When I was born my father, a tariff man, was temporarily estranged from his lifetime political hero and mine, President Stephen Grover Cleveland. The reason was that the President, in his annual message to Congress in 1887, had assailed the practice and principle of the protective tariff by proposing the near free-trade formula of the Mills Bill (which passed the House but died in the Senate). My father had once met President Chester Alan Arthur, and, apparently as an expression of his lingering resentment over the Mills Bill, I was named Arthur. By election time in 1888 my father had renewed his support of Cleveland, but it was too late to restore my handle to Grover C. as I believe was the original intention.

Why I was given the middle name (long since dropped) of Bernard I never knew for sure: there was nothing ancestral about it. But my father knew a citizen of Fredericksburg, Virginia, who in my hearing he described as the beau ideal of the Tidewater Virginia gentleman. And *his* name was Arthur Bernard.

Chapter Six

In a household which included eight sons and several grandsons, on land at the edge of a small town and extending into the country, it was inevitable that a host of domestic animals and some creatures from the wild would be part of the family establishment. Our menagerie, when I was growing up in Barren County, Kentucky, in the Nineties, was composed of numerous dogs, as many caged raccoons and possums, a brace of talkative and insolent crows, a gamecock, horses for the plough, the vehicle and the saddle, and now and then an indignant incarcerated fox. Such cats as there were among the occupants of this zoo lived in "the Quarters" (where "the help" resided), along with several foxhounds. The cats were the working members of the animal kingdom, the gendarmes of rodent control.

That *Ivanhoe* was the inspiration of our tiltings derived more from Mark Twain than from the Waverley Novels. But these and Sir Walter's poetry were favorites we sampled with equal relish, and even Sir Wilfred of Ivanhoe was no greater hero than Roderick Dhu. "Come one, come all!" we declaimed. "This rock shall fly/ From its firm base as soon as I" — providing ourselves with the indicated backstop. So popular a hero was the rebel chieftain of *The Lady of the Lake* that his name was bestowed on pets throughout the county. Hence it was most appropriate, "in," and timely for my champion gamecock to be named for him.

Roderick Dhu was famous in the land, and justly so, for four reasons, the fourth being unique in my knowledge of his gallant species. He could, and did, wage victorious battle against any rooster he encountered in the area. He could, and did, husband all our hens and those of other citizens, being received with every mark of appreciation by the tittering beneficiaries of his haughty favor. He could, and did, crow loud and shrill, not only at dawn, but whenever his sense of timing impelled him to. But, fourth, Roderick detested the company of his species and shunned it except for amorous visitations. Instead, he selected the house as his general abode, and, after several efforts to lodge him at night in the roost outside, he was allowed his preference.

This raised an obvious problem. But both my grandmother and Roderick were equal to it. She put a sand-filled box in an open closet off the kitchen, explained its purpose to Roderick with magic words

incomprehensible to any but the two principals, and
thence he never failed to repair when seized by certain natural urges.

I have known many roosters on varying terms of
intimacy, even participated in making available to
gamecocks the opportunity to indulge their congenital love of combat. But Roderick Dhu was the only
one with which I was acquainted or heard about that
nominated himself to be a member of a household
and learned to be acceptable in every way.

This noble bird lived long, happily and fruitfully.
And when the common summons of all earthlings
came, he met it with dignity and taste: he was found
dead on the seat of my deceased grandfather's special chair. His age, as nearly as we could calculate,
was thirteen. He was buried, with the honors he de-
served, in my grandmother's flower garden, under a
rosebush.

Bull Rock was about twelve years old when he
was imported to Virginia from England in 1730 to
stand at stud. His multitudinous progeny inaugurated the great expansion in the breeding and racing
of thoroughbreds that now are a leading American
industry-cum-sport. But for various reasons, among
them the facts that the eighteenth century's westering
pioneers brought thoroughbreds with them over the
mountains, and found the limestone water and blue-

grass pasture of Kentucky ideal to the purpose, our Commonwealth supplanted Virginia as the capital of the blood horse and has continued to be.

Though the Kentucky Bluegrass area, centered in Fayette, Bourbon, Franklin, Scott and Woodford counties, is the royal seat of the thoroughbred, all but the mountain areas of the state are his provinces, and my native Barren County was one of them. Poor indeed — or, if not poor, certainly queer in our sight — was the family which possessed no horse with at least an asserted trace of the blood of Bull Rock, Sir Archy, Priam, Bonnie Scotland or Lexington. And since we were neither poor nor eccentric enough to be bereft of the inbred Kentucky love of horses, I grew up with several which remain in loving memory.

The irony is, however, that the best-blooded of these did not return my love. He was Selim — an Arab, as his name suggests, purported to be descended from Admiral Tryon's Asil, which won the Newmarket in the 1770's. My uncles used him as a saddle horse, which was something beneath his dignity. Yet, as if he were familiar with certain maxims in Al Koran, he usually submitted to this use without the snorting, kicking and rearing that at times seemed to derive from a subconscious recollection of great stake races won by his ancestors.

My silly head crammed with "Mazeppa," "The Leap of Rushan Beg" and such poetic glorifications of the Arab horse, I was distressed to be informed by my uncles that Selim was a gelding. And, since I had assured all the boys in town that he was a stallion straight out of *The Arabian Nights*, I had to endure a certain amount of ribbing when the evident truth was pointed out.

Gelding or no, in aggressiveness toward horses of humbler lineage, in beauty of pace and form on the road, Selim was conceded by the local experts (and they were many and they were good) to be "a lot of horse." His eventual acquiescence, therefore, to a utilitarian duty in his and my grandfather's old age was an abiding wonder in our community. This duty was to transport my grandfather in our surrey to and from his place of business several times a day.

Somehow appearing to understand the necessity of the condescension — my grandfather having grown quite lame — Selim allowed himself to be harnessed and backed within the shafts of the surrey. Led to the gate, he would stand quietly until his passenger — whom he loved above all others — painfully made his way aboard the front seat. Then, without any direction of the reins, he would trot gently to the stile in front of my grandfather's office-store, and, after ascertaining his charge had safely debarked, return with the empty carriage to his stable until the hour came to fetch his master — a timetable which Selim knew and observed precisely.

This was my first case of unrequited love, though Ovidian in nature. But in my own old age I still cherish the consolation that in his last years Selim had come briefly to tolerate the laying of my hand on his imperial neck.

I do not remember any of the cats specifically. None was admitted to the house, and it was not until much later in my life that I learned to appreciate these animals — their fascinating mixture of love and indifference, and the rippling beauty of their muscular construction. Not until the time I had become a newspaper executive in Louisville, and had a young family and a house of my own, did my association and love for cats begin, with a drifter named Grimalkin.

The line ended in Washington and Virginia in the Nineteen Forties with two extraordinary felines: a Siamese of imperial lineage which we called Puss-Pants because her name in Mandarin that Rosamond Pinchot gave her in the cattery was too long for calling and too Chinese to pronounce; and James Mc-Near, a short-haired Persian, a very great gentleman.

The dogs of my childhood were: a pack of St. Bernards, both short- and long-haired, varying in number because Moxie and Princess, the matriarchs, produced large litters with the cooperation of Kaintuck, long-haired, a prolific sire and a London dog-show winner; Nero, a black Newfoundland; a hassle of hounds of the chase; and Bright. This Bright, a short-haired fox terrier, a feist if ever there was one, took advantage of his size to tyrannize over the St. Bernards. He was further encouraged by some members of the family in his outrageous performances — snarling at the big dogs when they foolishly made kind advances, stealing from their meat bowls, and yapping shrilly when they were being caressed by his master, my best friend, beloved mentor and companion, Dan Smiley.

Dan was a tall, sinewy man with the disposition of an angel. He took care of the family's needs in a number of outdoor capacities and was available for light butlering, too. Insofar as the boys of the household were concerned he was the most important of all. He was deeply versed in the lore of the field and the forest: he instructed us all how to "ride, shoot and draw the bow" — those "three useful things" which, according to Byron, were taught by the ancient Persians. Dan's cabin in the backyard was our favorite gathering place. And, though not at all resembling the drawings of Uncle Remus that adorned the immortal book by Joel Chandler Harris, he was a spinner of tales about the creatures in the animal kingdom that moved us into a state of bliss. So that Bright, when he appointed himself as Dan Smiley's special dog, acquired an undeserved prestige he unpleasantly made the most of.

Dan Smiley was a genius in the rearing and handling of dogs, hunting dogs in general and foxhounds in particular. Since Barren County, under the leadership of Colonel Haiden C. Trigg, a banker and our leading citizen, was the breeding center for the hounds in which the Walker and Trigg strains were fused, Dan's talent made him a very respected member of the community. Eventually, when our household dispersed to the four winds, he was appointed kennelman-in-chief for the Barren County pack. And when he died in the fullness of years, the whole community and hunters from afar followed his casket to the grave. Of all those present none mourned more deeply than I — not for the gifted sportsman, but for the friend, teacher and gentle patron of my lost youth.

I have mentioned the sire of our St. Bernard, Kaintuck, and that he once won a prize in a dog show in London — taken there by my Uncle Ed, to whom his ownership was reluctantly conceded. Among us he was familiarly known as Tuck, and he lived long and beneficently. When my uncle moved his family to

Summer Shade, in Metcalfe County, sixteen miles from Glasgow, I missed Tuck so much that I paid repeated visits to that village. And our reunions were joyous, for, though all his breed are suffused with affection, Tuck's ebullience in greeting was the most complimentary in my experience with a host of dogs.

There were certain hazards involved when close to a hundred pounds of rearing dog bore down his large paws on the shoulders of a seventy-pound boy and licked his face with a tongue which flowed like Philemon's pitcher, practically inundating the object of his love. No such problems arose when Tuck joined me as my sleeping companion in the feather bed my Aunt Julia allotted to me. He was a most considerate bedfellow. His first idea of this relationship was expressed by getting under the cover with me. But, effectively discouraged by my aunt when she discovered Tuck's head on the pillow, he consented thereafter to sleep *on* the cover at the foot. In our outdoor ramblings, he needed no lesson in discipline. For, except when we accidentally flushed a quail, or another dog indicated a challenge of the right-of-way, Tuck behaved with dignified reserve.

This manner he maintained even at the cockfights which in my boyhood were a Sunday morning diversion of Summer Shade — after church. But once I thought Tuck carried dignity too far, considering that St. Bernards are supposed to be — and usually are — the guardians of youth from exterior danger and interior folly.

My best friend in Summer Shade was Cleveland Word, who lived on a farm which it was my delight to visit. On the occasion I speak of, we were exploring the barn and came upon a large sack of bran. It being well known to us that cattle found bran delicious, we decided to share their pleasure, and washed down a goodly quantity of the feed with large draughts of water. Tuck lay languidly watching as we ate and drank, for which I reproached him when, inevitably, the combination of bran and water expanded violently in our stomachs and we twisted on the barn floor in pain.

It wasn't too long until nature relieved us with a visceral explosion that seemed powerful enough to blow the roof off the barn. Only then did Tuck indicate concern. But this was the one time in our long and loving relationship that he failed to live up to the reputation of the all-round protector of children which legend attributes to his species.

CHAPTER SEVEN

ALTHOUGH THE VILLAGE of Summer Shade was only sixteen miles from Glasgow, the journey thereto by public transportation consumed a whole forenoon in normal weather conditions. And this public transportation was the fulfillment of a boy's dream — a bright-red stagecoach with yellow wheels, drawn by four chestnut horses! Its regular run was from Glasgow, east by south, to Burkesville, the seat of Cumberland County, on the Tennessee line, Summer Shade being a stop on the way.

I still recall the thrill which suffused my being when, with Tom Shelby or his brother at the reins, the gleaming coach drew up to load this small passenger for a journey made even more adventurous by the facts that Burkesville Road was a deeply rutted streak of red clay, and there was always a chance that the fords of Boyd's, Skaggs's and Fallen Timber creeks would mire the coach in their sandy bottoms, or be covered by flash floods. In the latter event only the expertness of the Shelby brothers could prevent the coach from being swept into deep water.

On all the occasions of my visits to Summer Shade, however, whichever of these hazards that developed was safely negotiated. But once I decided to return to Glasgow by another means of transportation, a lumber wagon without springs. It was a day's ride, and my bottom retained painful memories of it for at least a week.

I do not know whether the Barren County Hunt has since acquired the pink coats of the chase that were set in the English tradition as proper equipment for all but the huntsman and the farmers who opened their land to the sport. Nor do I know whether the Virginia gentlemen in the seventeenth and eighteenth centuries, who rode out after the fox from Westover, Shirley, Carter's Grove or the two Brandons, included pink coats in the raiment they ordered from London.

But fox-hunting in Barren County in my boyhood involved neither the traditional English dress nor the galloping after Reynard until he was "viewed," "found," "killed" or "stole away." The hunters would assemble on horseback in the twilight, at a given place, bringing the hounds along in carts and wagons; also a generous supply of bourbon whiskey. They would then proceed to the top of a hill commanding the topography, leaving the hounds and their handlers at the foot. Moonrise was the ideal time for the hunt to begin as soon as an accommodating fox was viewed or scented by the hounds and handlers below. Then, with ears attuned to the music of the horn and the racing pack, the hunters would fall to pleasant drinking until the hunt below culminated one way or another.

This leisurely sport, fox-hunting only for the hounds and those who handled them, usually lasted until moonset. Which was taken as sufficient explanation for the absence now and then of married members of the hunt who were notoriously henpecked.

Not until a boy reached his middle teens was he likely to be allowed to join the men on the hilltop or the kennelmen below, not so much because the so-called hunt took place at night as because much whiskey was consumed. But boys needed only their parents' permission to join in the hunt for the possum and the coon, and these were far more enjoyable experiences. Moreover, the boys, black and white, were essential participants because they often were on terms of greater intimacy with the coon and possum dogs than most of their elders.

One of my happiest remembrances is the sharp barking which announced the treeing of either of these creatures — the coon with bared teeth challenging the dogs to try sampling them; the possum, eyes closed, stretched out motionless in the treetop pretending to be dead. I never saw one get away with this act: his fate was to finish in a pot where he steamed along with yams or sweet potatoes to make a meal as succulent to our palates as any entrée could be to the patrons of a three-star restaurant in Paris. But many possums and more coons eluded the hunters and the dogs by other employments of the inherent cunning of the small marsupial and the daring of the ring-tailed arboreal carnivore.

My favorite sport, however, was the hunting of the quail: alternately we called them bobwhites and they were plentiful in the country. My usual starting point was the residence of an older friend, Bryan Strader, at Hiseville, a village ten miles from Glasgow. The hunt was preceded by the hospitality of a fine supper and bed for the night, and at five A.M. we would set out with shotguns and bird dogs in search of the coveys. With average good luck we could count on a full bag, yet within a sportsman's limit, sometimes after ten miles of walking. Not until, many years later, I hunted quail on horseback in South Carolina did I realize that the sport involved anything less than sheer, though very worthwhile, fatigue.

CHAPTER EIGHT

AMONG THE OMNIUM, undescriptive labels
which corrupt the English language, per-
haps "white" and "black" are the falsest. It is not my
affair that spokesmen for many of those Americans
of African ancestry have induced them to refer to
themselves as "blacks," despite the fact that this was
the contemptuous word of the slave traders and the
alien colonizers. But I am even more puzzled by the
American Black Moslems and their adopted names
of Ali, Mohammed and the like. For it was Arab
Moslems who founded the trade of selling Africans
into slavery.

In the ethnic divisions of that place and time I am
describing, though the classification of Negroes covered all shades from very light to very black, from
octoroon and mulatto to "blue gum," they were generally lumped referentially as "colored." It was taken
by both groups as a dignified designation, and was
so intended. But even with respect to facial composition, tones of voice and pronunciation, the differences

among those of varying degrees of African origin were as varied as among the descendants of the early Teutons, Celts, Angles and their innumerable mixtures who make up the white majority. And it was among the colored citizens that, like many other boys, my greatest affections and companionships were centered.

With these my happiest hours were spent: with Dan Smiley, with "Aunt" Courtney and "Uncle" Armistead, with Easter and Perry Wells, with Isom and Virgil.

Aunt Courtney was my mammy. At her breast she had suckled the puling infant my mother could not nourish until my grandmother's experiments demonstrated that I could be salvaged on oatmeal. With that discovery I emerged from the shadow of death into a healthy baby. My survival thus assured, Aunt Courtney concentrated on "bringing me up," according to her high standards of gentility, with a combination of tenderness and discipline that bound us in love to the day she died. Her husband, Uncle Armistead, and she were both magnificent creatures — tall, ebony-black, strong physically, with broad brows and noses, proud in their carriage.

They were born slaves, and had small education, but they knew whence and how they came to human servitude in an alien land. They were of the warrior tribe of the Amazulu whose impis (regiments), armed but with spears, used to shake the earth as they went into battle, and, in the days of their great king Chaka, had Caucasian soldiers retreating more than once. Aunt Courtney and Uncle Armistead had been told by their parents that, defeated in battle, their ancestors had been captured and sold by the victors to Arab slave-traders, who in turn sold them into the bondage that began with transport to the American colonies in the floating hells of that shameful era.

Obviously, I cannot faithfully reproduce the narrative of these events as told to me more than seventy years ago. Nor shall I attempt to do more than indicate the dialect and the syntax of Uncle Armistead as he unfolded the tale to a boy aglow with Rider Haggard's tales of the exploits of *Allan Quatermain*. But it went something like this:

"Must have been my grandpappy, maybe the one befo' him, in Firginny, that 'splained whar we come from. But he said we was always big people, with big heads and faces, like you see us now, and any of our menfolks could kill a lion with a spear if he could git close enough. But land and water — that's what we was always needin' and always had to fight for with the trash that tried to keep us from gittin' em: they was called the Matabele.

"Well, it seems one time we got us a sorry [worthless] king who liked likker and women better than lookin' after his kingdom, and when he ambushed the wife of a Matabele king and run off with 'er it started a war. Most of our fightin' men had got fat and lazy under this sorry king of ours, though they were nacherly as brave as they come, so we lost the war and got took captive. The Matabele sold us, men, women and childern, for slaves to those brown-skins on the coast, Arabs who call de Lawd 'Olivah' [Allah], and the next thing my folks knew we was crossin' big water in the hold of a ship, and chained together so's we couldn't hardly move a muscle. We landed around New Orleans somewhere, was sold off to the plantations, and your Aunt Courtney and me ended up on one in Firginny as children and was sold off together into Kintucky. Thar we got married, and the good Jesus saw to it that we had a good marster until Mr. Linkum give us our freedom."

Whenever I hungered for something very special, after Aunt Courtney had retired from our service, I would go to her house. And not in any of the great restaurants in many lands that I know have I encountered a cuisine which seemed to me more delicious. Perhaps it requires a Southern taste and upbringing to arrive at this judgment. But if there are viands more grateful to the palate than her gumbo, hoecake, ashcake, johnnycake, corn pone, jowl-and-greens, hominy samp and grits, fried ham and chicken, chocolate cream pie, black-eyed peas with bacon — any of these — I have not found them.

Many of the same delights of the palate were always available to me at the house of Aunt Easter and Uncle Perry Wells. This hospitality was the highest civility of the area and the period. The Wellses, too, like most of the adult Negroes in our community, had first seen the light in slave quarters, and, young as I was, I understood what their freedom and that of their children meant to them. Aunt Easter was our seamstress; and occasionally, when the size and nature of the entertaining called for escalation of our simple dining routine, she helped in the preparation and service of the food. As for Uncle Perry, the farm he and his family owned and worked had been made possible by my grandfather: he gave a part of the price for the land and equipment and loaned the rest at, of course, no interest.

On the occasions when I let it be known, in what I fear was lordly fashion, that I was in a mood to sample the cooking, I would arrive to find a table covered by a gleaming white cloth and a single chair drawn up to it. But, though the children of the household were not permitted to dine with even so unworthy a member of the master race as I, they would stand around and watch me devour every morsel. This undoubtedly whetted their appetites for the special dishes they would shortly inherit.

So far as I was concerned I would gladly have
eaten in their company. But to my hostesses this
would have been a violation of their protocol, founded
in a pride which one who was not brought up by Negro women in the South of my childhood could not
be expected to comprehend. The protocol did not extend to any other association: my most enjoyable
companions, because of their congenital gaiety, and
inventive and physical skills, were the very ones
whom their mothers would not permit to sit with me
at table.

This companionship ended when I reached high-
school age — an automatic response to the accepted
customs of the society to which both groups belonged.
But the custom had its exceptions; it did not reach to
the close relations thereafter between, for example,
Dan Smiley and me. And until my boyhood was past
this was also my relationship with Virgil.

Virgil's shade was so black that it verged on deep
blue; but the expression "blue gum" also meant that
Negroes of this complexion usually lived in the
thickets where the eucalyptus tree grew. I suppose a
game that he and I played constantly was my own
idea, but at any rate he was as enthusiastic a partici-
pant as I. It consisted of laying a chair on its back,
harnessing to it either Virgil or one of the St. Bernards — usually the matriarch Princess because of
her amiability, strength and intelligence — and ca-

reening over the lawn. I was always a passenger, and I reserved the right to decide on each occasion whether my riding companion was to be Virgil or Princess.

There was a risk involved because of my grandmother's stern disapproval of the performance. If she discovered us, some punitive price had to be paid: Virgil and I were not allowed to play with each other for a fixed period — usually a day or so — during which Princess was kept within eyesight of the house. The animation of my grandmother's disapproval was in this order: I was subjecting a noble beast and a faithful retainer to indignity.

But after the second time the penalty was imposed it occurred to me there was a simple way to keep on with the game and go undiscovered. This was to borrow a kitchen knife, announcing in my grandmother's hearing that we were going to the field across the road to cut and eat sugar cane, ask and receive permission for Princess to go with us, and, safely away from the purview of the house, unearth an old chair we had hidden in the field and activate our chariot in the meadow beyond the cane.

When we wearied of the game, or it came under the ban, there were many happy alternatives. One was to go swimming in South Fork Creek that flowed at the end of the property, where Virgil was a strict teacher and I a backward pupil. On a return to Glasgow for a visit in my early twenties I sought out Virgil only to find that he had infracted the law and was temporarily behind stone walls in a distant town. Many experiences in my life have saddened me, but at that period none more so than the loss of this merry companion. For he did not come back, and I never saw him again.

The simple security measures in our town were much less official than based on voluntary assistance of neighbor to neighbor. Most important of these was a volunteer fire department. The fire engine hose-cart was hand-drawn. When a fire broke out the crew rushed the machine to the scene of action where, under the direction of my Uncle Louis, the commander, the blaze was put out whenever the hose was long enough to reach the nearest water supply. Often, after I was twelve years old or so, when I heard my uncle summoned to duty in the night, I would join him in the stable where he was saddling his thoroughbred, Lady Belle, and ride another horse to the fire. On the last occasion of this kind I found the experience fairly expensive.

The fire had drawn a crowd of onlookers; my presence was especially noted because I signified the return of the native, having by then been a reporter in Louisville for a couple of years. As I rode along with the crowd a cluster of black and brown hands pulled gently at my stirrup, their owners informing me, "I was named for you." To have failed to present each namesake with a small coin would have been a betrayal of my caste. Fortunately I had not removed the silver from my pants pockets when I went to bed. But I think I was out about five dollars, a big bite in my salary of fifteen dollars a week in Louisville.

Among the most fascinating characters in the country were the Negro preachers, at camp meetings of the faithful, where they prophesied fell disease as the immediate, and an eternal environment of fire and brimstone after death as the eventual punishment for sinners. I doubt whether the Reverend Billy Graham ever brought more recruits per capita to the mourners' bench than these preachers at the Negro camp meetings. And no evangelist ever surpassed them in their oratory, with respect to its instant effects on the penitent.

One of the most accomplished of these preachers was Theophilus (I have forgotten his surname). His thundering bass, both in speech and the singing of spirituals, was not matched by any of his fellow shepherds of the erring, whose mission was to convince them they had strayed from the narrow path of righteousness. Although the talents of Theophilus in the pulpit left no reasonable doubt of the validity of his vocation, it was a matter of debate how he had recognized it. For he, when not describing hell in a detail which scared my companions and me into temporary good behavior, was a wholly illiterate field hand.

Aware that his ascension to the ministry on Sundays was something of a mystery to the entire community, he disposed of the dubiety by his opening remarks to the first sermon he preached. "You all," he said (I am indicating rather than precisely recording the dialect), "knows I got a mule. You knows I ploughs with this mule in the backbreakin' toil which is his lot and mine. Well, one day this mule turned round in his harness and opened his mouf and brayed. Well, it warn't like your usual mule-brayin', so it took me some time to figure it out. Then it come to me. This mule was sayin' 'Oh, Theophilus: go PREE-ACH, go PREE-ch, go PREE-ch!' And I knowed it was God and Jesus callin' me, to put sich a call in the mouf of my mule. And I reesponded to the Call, accordin' to which I am here in this pulpit today."

Our elders laughed, but we boys did not. And never was a mule so much the observed of all observers as when he and Theophilus opened the rocky soil to fruitfulness. But, though the mule often made the music of his species in our hearing, and we were unable to fit it to the words which Theophilus heard, we accepted the explanation as merely another proof that God moves in a mysterious way his wonders to perform.

It was customary at these camp meetings for a member of the congregation to discuss with the preacher some doubt of Holy Writ which was nagging at his faith. Occasionally a question of this kind would stump a reverend. But not Theophilus.

One Sunday the following Q and A occurred after a sermon in which Theophilus assured his hearers of the absolute infallibility of the Bible:

Q. You says that when the Prophet Jacob, layin' on that rock in the desert, was woken up by a shinin' light from Heaven, he see a big passel of God's angels ascendin' and condescendin' a big ladder that reached up to where God was settin'. You says it's in the Bible and must therefoh be so.

A. I says that, the Bible says that, and it true.

Q. Reverend, cain't angels fly?

A. Co'se they can.

Q. Then why was them angels ascendin' and condescendin' the ladder on their feet?

A. They was moltin'.

That ended this venture into the Higher Criticism. And the colloquy was one of many, in which Theophilus had a crushing explanation for any doubt of Holy Writ that was raised.

The old-time fundamental religious persuasion that the camp meetings revealed was a most important source of the good citizenship that dominated the Negro as well as the white members of the community. This good citizenship was expressed in compassion for the unfortunate, a stress on public order and a common front against adversity.

The hard-shell (hard-side) Baptists, black and white, firmly believed that total immersion was the only baptismal rite which assured entrance into a state of grace, and that instrumental church music (especially the organ) was a lure of Satan. The Methodists believed that sprinkling was adequate baptism in the sight of the Lord, and were a little more lenient where church music was concerned. The "Campbellites," followers of Alexander Campbell (their churches were called "Christian," as if this was an exclusive possession), adhered to the doctrines of predestination and redemption of the spirit, but less rigidly so than the Presbyterians.

Since there were only a handful of Catholic families (descendants of those English folk who accompanied Lord Calvert and Lord Baltimore to the Maryland colony) there were services at their little church about once a month. The priest was borrowed from the pioneer Catholic community of Bardstown, in Nelson County, where rose the first cathedral west of the Alleghenies, and east of the Spanish communities in the Far West, that became a part of the United States. As aforenoted, there was no synagogue.

But religion, and especially the Negro gatherings, including the camp meetings, were an enormous influence in establishing and preserving what was best in the mores of the community. The so-called "holiness sects" were not successful in their periodic attempts to invest the Christian worship with their fanaticism. But they, too, contributed to the maintenance of the substantial social values (however the Higher Criticism may deride them) of what was known as a God-fearing community.

Among the mysteries of man's creation, the cortex which surrounds that part of the brain where memory lies is one of the most awesome. It is from this gray envelope, I suppose, that one can reassemble the sights, sounds and their environment which have lain fallow for decades. Only in this way can I explain why, as I think back on the camp meetings in my youth, the words, the melodies, and even the marvelous orchestration of Negro voices that is unmatched by any of the other races of man, recur almost fully in my mind.

Many of the spirituals are now widely familiar, and there are numerous collections of them. But some that I heard as a boy are not to be found in the books known to me: perhaps they were native to that part of the country and did not travel. Among these:

I'm a Baptist born and a Baptist bred,
And when I die there'll be a Baptist dead.
And when I goes to heaven there'll be a happy time,
A-eatin' of the honey and a-drinkin' of the wine.

Jine that golden band, jine that golden band.
Ef you don't jine that golden band
Gwine-a hit you on the head with a golden axe.

———

My brother and my sister don't you talk-a dat way,
Walk on Jerusalem woe.
For the night am dark and I cannot stay,
Walk on Jerusalem woe.
For the night am dark and the road am rough,
Walk on Jerusalem woe.
Ef you tries you git dar sho e-nuf,
Walk on Jerusalem woe.
Lawd, I'm gwine
Yes I'm gwine,
Deed I'm gwine
To walk on Jerusalem woe.

———

I want to be an angel
And with the angels stand,

A crown upon my forehead,
A harp within my hand.

In the white community also there were songs I
have never heard elsewhere. They were not what
the entrepreneurs of Nashville have since popular-
ized, and thereby enriched themselves, as "country
music," though their origin actually was in the
backwoods and the hills. One was pure rude nonsense:

Tom Wilson is a walkin' man,
Nobody walkin' like he can,
From Pruitt's Knob to Bowling Green,
Like of him was never seen.
Walk Tom Wilson, walk.
Walk Tom Wilson, walk.
Walk Tom Wilson, afternoon;
Sweep that kitchen with a brand-new broom. . . .
He combed his head with a wagon wheel
And died with a toothache in his heel.

Another concerned jiggling a child on an elder's
knee, its purpose being to replace an outburst of
tears with laughter. For me this transformation of
mood was always achieved when my grandfather
sang:

Rain come wet me, sun come dry me,
Git away black man, don't you come a-nigh me.

> Hello, gals, give me chaw terbacker;
> Hello, boys, give me drink of whiskey,
> When I'm drunk then I'm frisky —
> Yiddy, yiddy eye-do aye.

I never was aware that the second line carried implications of the attitude that now would be denounced as "racist," since I never connected it with our Negro community. Nor, I am sure, did so practical a sympathizer with the victims of slavery and gross discrimination as my grandfather was: acting on his own, he had freed his slaves in the late Eighteen Forties, put them on wages, and otherwise helped many Negroes attain economic status and personal dignity thereafter. To him, as to me, this was just a jingle — its innocent intent merely to dry my tears.

Fragments of other songs of that time and place are all that I remember, such as:

> See that boat come round the bend,
> Goodbye, my lover, goodbye,
> Laden down with Kentucky men,
> Goodbye, my lover, goodbye.

> By, baby, bye-oh,
> By, baby, bye-oh,
> By, baby, bye-oh,
> Goodbye, my lover, goodbye.

I got a gal, she lives in Letcher*
She won't come and I won't fetch her . . .

Tennessee gals are handsome,
And Georgia gals are sweet,
But there's a gal in old Kaintucky —
She's the one I want to meet.

In relating that all the servants in a community such as ours were Negroes, I merely state a social fact of the time and place. But I recall one aspect of their service that gave me, young as I was and inured to the civilization I grew up in, a strong sense of discomfort. The sense was stronger because the servitors were my friends and playmates, once we were outdoors.

In this period there were no screens for the doors and windows, and in the long hot seasons the flies were a great annoyance. So two Negro boys, equipped with small tree branches, were stationed at either end of the table where we took our meals, their task being to wave the branches constantly to ward off the persistent flies. I knew that in India these attendants were known to the British as punka-coolies; and, Mr. Kipling having assured me that

* Letcher is a Kentucky mountain county.

this was a fitting convenience to the master race in
its pursuit of benevolent improvement of the "lesser
breeds without the law," I took some comfort in the
imperialist precedent. But it bothered me, and I was
very glad when we acquired screens, which supplanted the need for the human fly-swatters.

The service at meals was simple: in my halcyon
days the food was brought in by a colored friend,
hardly more than a boy, named Isom, and my grandmother filled and passed the laden plates, which were
passed in turn by each receiver. On special occasions
my grandfather (and, after his death, an elder
uncle) carved the main course if it was that sort of
viand. And, though table manners were strictly enforced (my grandmother's discipline consisting of
smacking any offender's hand within reach with the
sharp ivory nails of a long ebony backscratcher),
some latitude was permitted in competition for a
drumstick or another desirable part of the anatomy
of the entrée.

Another special privilege that came within the
regulations was extended on Sundays when ice
cream topped the menu. This privilege consisted in
being allowed to lick the dasher, the central mechanical unit in old-fashioned freezers. But eligibility de-
pended on which claimant had turned the handle
of the freezer the longest. The rivalry was intense,
but only among a few, because to the others the

privilege seemed hardly worth the toil required to win it.

In a rude fashion Isom performed, I suppose, the duties of a butler, though I do not recall that the term was ever employed in our simple household. Nevertheless, this was his function, and, well trained at our table, Isom — as sort of homespun caterer — eventually made a career of it, on call for any occasion when a member of the community, as our vernacular had it, "put on the dog." After several decades, during which I did not revisit Glasgow, I returned during the Fifties to see my two surviving aunts there. It was around the Thanksgiving holiday, and so my Aunt Anne (Redding) ordered a midday dinner appropriate to the season. Since she had invited a group of men and women I had grown up with, extra helping hands in the kitchen and at the table were necessary.

Once the company was seated, in strode a gray-haired butler in a white coat, who began majestically to supervise the service of a couple of aproned young women. Our eyes met, but he made no sign of recognition: Jeeves himself, at Blandings, could not have faulted this butler's impeccable demeanor. But it broke down when, calling his name, I got up from the table and put my arms around him. For this paragon of itinerant majordomos was Isom. And when the company dispersed, after nostalgic exchanges about happenings in the days of our youth, Isom, his wife Isabel (also a childhood friend), who had cooked the dinner, and I had a reunion which delayed my departure.

My wife, who was born and reared in Lake Forest, Illinois, was both pleased and touched by the relationship thus revealed. Nevertheless, I think she did not quite understand it. Not because of any arrogance of breed, but because she had known only white servants, and never their children, in the households of her parents and grandparents; and the tenderness of association thus revealed by me, inherent in the South in my day, simply does not seem to have crossed the broad Ohio.

As I drove out of Glasgow, to resume a journey whose destination was Corpus Christi, Texas, where lived my wife's older son and his family, I was thinking less of the familiar scenery I was traversing than the object lesson I had just experienced of the American wanderlust which had replaced the durable community of kinfolk of my childhood. For these two aunts were all that remained in Barren County of the large Morris clan. The rest of the elders lay either in the town graveyard or in the disparate earths of Louisville, Chicago, Seattle, Eufaula, Alabama, New Orleans and Vancouver, Canada.

In passing the Morris Block on the Square, where

my grandfather's office-store had been, and after his
death that of his son Gus and James Depp, a partner,
I noticed that only the name on the lintel of the front
entrance recalled the original builder. Wordsworth's
line, had I remembered it, would have aptly described my meditations: "Homeless near a thousand
homes."

The affectionate childhood relationship in Glasgow between blacks and whites existed among the
adults, too. It stopped at the point of dining together
and other social intermingling. But the elders of my
family and their grown-up sons and daughters numbered Negroes among their closest and most faithful
friends and returned the friendship, each adult group
in its own particular fashion. The Negroes served,
yes, but also they were called into conference on
equal terms on matters affecting the household, agri-
culture, and the security of the community from
racial violence. For at least in our community, the
responsible Negroes possessed in exceptional measure the instinct for wise solutions of such problems.

My grandmother, as aforesaid, had a proverb
to fit many situations derived, I suppose, subconsciously from the experiences of ancestors in the distant abyss of time. But the Negroes quoted proverbs
that were guidelines for every conceivable perplexity,
some from the Bible but some from folklore more

ancient. I recall only a few, cudgel my brain as I may, but they include: "Ef hit had been a snake he would have bit you" (referring to a search for something that lay in plain view). "De Lawd don't have to wear no specs to see a sinner at his sinning" (a prediction that punishment for error was as certain as the rising of the sun). "Don't lay no money on de debbil rovin' about like a ragin' lion: he is mo' liable to snuck up on you as a lamb."

There were cruelty and neglect in our community, of which the Negroes were among the victims. And some businessmen and farmers cheated those of both races who could not read or who were afraid to complain of disregard of the axiom that the laborer is worthy of his hire. Also, of course, as in all Southern areas, there were white men who used Negro women and cast them and their halfbreed babies heartlessly aside. But insofar as I could observe — allowing for the fact that I left Glasgow in my youth — these were exceptional cases, and the white community expressed its disapproval in several effective ways such as denying hospitality to offenders — a radical measure indeed in the South of my time.

One custom was that young unmarried women would "sit for company" on Sundays, with all callers writing their names in what was known as a chapbook. But, as a typical example of community disapproval, it was made clear to men who exploited the Negroes that they were not welcome.

I come reluctantly to make use of the ratings, copied by the American from the British press, by which population groups are crudely lumped as the upper, middle, lower middle and working classes. The descriptions cannot possibly pass the test of accuracy, being both transitory and based on income; also this base is distasteful in a democracy. But I have searched in vain for substitute terms to describe the standing of the responsible Negroes in our community in the Eighteen Nineties, and must settle for identifying them as the lower middle class in a society that was essentially all middle except for a few families which traced their ancestry to the English Colonial gentry.

Below this Negro group was the one accurately designated as "white trash" because they were social primitives in act, manners, education and character, with an ingrained distaste for regular work. And no whites, however high their station, scorned "white trash" more than did the fine Negro citizenry: indeed, it was they who coined the expression.

Yet we did not refer, in speech or print, to Negroes as "Mr." and "Mrs." and in public assemblage they sat apart. The detestable blight of slavery was also still manifest in such practices as segregated public transportation. I still remember the sense of shame I felt when, on a hot summer day, a Negro having boarded a crowded streetcar in Louisville and stood in the vestibule for a breath of air, one of my uncles ordered him to the rear.

CHAPTER NINE

I SPENT VERY LITTLE TIME in the local grammar school — the yield of the bad seed of infant ill-health, of the pampering which accompanies rearing by grandparents, and of a gift of ingenuity in devising excuses for absenteeism. Since the expense of childbirth was that my mother was blind for six years thereafter, and in the course of this affliction she joined my father who had got a job in Chicago, my grammar and secondary school "education" was divided geographically. But among the most vivid of my recollections of my schooling was the one-room structure in Glasgow where Miss Bybee introduced us to learning.

A gentle but firm teacher, with a culture beyond its humble point of distribution, she filled me, at least, with a zeal for seeking knowledge. Repulsively precocious, I had learned by the age of three how to tell time and memorize what was read to me (beginning with "The Dogs' Dinner-Party"). When I came under Miss Bybee's tutelage I had begun to read some polite fiction in my grandfather's library and bits of history and biography. On this foundation I acquired the beginnings of a mental discipline which, though too often breached in my case by a congenital indolence, is essential to what has become known in my trade as "reporting in depth."

Our classes were composed of boys and girls from the town and from the countryside — the range of the latter restricted by the availability of the transportation methods of the area and period. It was easy enough for town children to walk to school, but if the journey was above five miles or so, country children had to depend on any member of the family or neighbor who owned a horse or a mule. Holiday periods were largely in winter for climatic reasons, even though snow and ice were rare and brief visitations. So among my early remembrances is the pain of wrestling with the Rule of the Three R's (plus S for spelling) when the outdoors beckoned with special insistence.

Of my schoolmates in Glasgow I best recall Brice Leech, Waller Depp, Al Shirley, Joe Kilgore, Edgar Caldwell, a couple of the numerous sons of Colonel and Mrs. Trigg, the Lessenberry brothers and cousins, and several girls for whom I felt a deep but shifting affection.

It is neither fable nor folklore that the women of Kentucky are remarkable for their astonishing quota of exceptional beauties — usually fair-haired, blue-eyed and lissome of figure — and all particularly skilled in the art of reducing their admirers to a state of happy bondage. At one time or another I was thus enslaved by Kate Depp, Maud Lessenberry and the Bohannon twins, Charlotte and Caroline, while also adoring at a distance Kate's elder sister Minnie. Although she was my senior by three years, this barrier did not spare me the pangs of calf love, such as young Marchbanks suffered for Candida in the play by Shaw, when, on a homecoming visit, Minnie Depp drove me around the Square in her shiny new phaeton.

But "the proper study of mankind is man," and this study, being an essential part of true education, had a vast storehouse of references in a community such as that I grew up in and those I grew to know thereafter.

The aphorism that "alcohol and gasoline don't mix" was generated by the growing number of fatal traffic accidents for which drunken drivers are responsible. In my Glasgow boyhood — we had no internal combustion engines because there were as yet no automobiles in the community — a corollary aphorism could have been: "Southerners and alcohol, especially, don't mix."

For the native Southern breed in those days appears in retrospect to have had a special inclination to violence under the influence of alcohol. And, since Saturday night was by custom the time in Glasgow for drinking to excess, it was usually a violent occasion on the streets of town.

The town marshal, Winston Collins, was one of the gentlest men I ever knew. He maintained a remarkable degree of order by virtue of his courage, persuasiveness and the respect the community had for him. Yet, because of the intensity of the fire which alcohol lighted in the breasts of some of our normally peaceful citizens, it was Marshal Collins's bitter lot to be forced to use lethal methods in dealing with them on Saturday night. Otherwise, the public order and his life, as well as the lives of innocent bystanders, would have been the sacrifice.

It was the duty and function of Marshal Collins to forestall these recurring nights of violence, or, failing, to restore law and order by whatever means was necessary. And all too frequently this means was the Colt revolver, the "Peacemaker" of the Old West.

Most of the occasions when Marshal Collins was forced to draw on an offender or offenders, the badge of authority that gleamed on his chest, plus his reputation as a very fast gun and the respect and affection in which even the brawlers held him, were sufficient to end the violence, often with no more casualties than minor wounds. But when whiskey had inflamed beyond control one or another of the town's citizens or visitors, pacification and disarmament were extremely difficult and dangerous to attempt, the more so because the comparatively sober siblings and friends intervened.

So far as I could determine, and I always made it a point to see Marshal Collins in his old age on homecoming visits, he died with the serenity of mind that should attend awareness of a hard duty knowingly assumed and met in full.

Yet throughout this period of my boyhood Glasgow was a "dry" town and Barren was a "dry" county. For national prohibition merely lent emphasis to a condition precedent, which was that the racially mixed conglomerate society of the United States votes dry and drinks wet (principally whiskey) in the "Bible Belt."

Ecological conditions, found in more perfect balance for distilling corn in Kentucky than elsewhere in the United States, account for the fact that straight bourbon whiskey is the finest product of the kind anywhere in the world. Its base is the purity of water when strained through deposits of limestone, and careful aging of raw bourbon by generations of distillers has steadily perfected it. But because, from early times in the life of the nation, the Federal government has drawn a large annual revenue by taxing whiskey, evasion of the tax by moonshiners has led to the circulation in the South of a raw spirit of a nature highly inflammatory to the emotions of its imbibers, and especially provocative of a congenital tendency to violence.

This illegal moonshine whiskey — known variously as "white lightning" and "white mule" — was always in full supply in the community, particularly on Saturday nights. There was also aged bourbon to be had illegally, but this was much more costly. The moonshine came from stills, movable from one location to another when Federal "revenooers" demolished them or got too close for continued production.

The aged bourbon was acquired from drugstores by medical prescriptions, although few were bona-fide issues of the physicians by whom they were purported to have been signed. For in our community the practicing doctors met the highest standards of the Hippocratic oath and professional capacity.

So outstanding were Glasgow's physicians that I vividly remember five, down to their very lineaments and turns of speech. One was Dr. Leech, who amiably endured the obvious pun evoked by the connection of his name and his profession. He encouraged me to extend my reading to the natural sciences. And whenever I met him on the street in the company of someone unknown to me, he invariably introduced me as "a member of one of Glasgow's oldest families" — an acknowledgment on which he and I both set store.

Three of the other physicians who live in my memory were Dr. Trabue, Dr. Grinstead and Dr. Garnett. Like Dr. Leech they were men of great dignity and compassion, holding themselves committed to answer any call for help, from persons however humble, without regard to race and however distant and difficult the journey to their bedsides. But my closest relations, of course, were with our family G.P., Dr. Jepson.

He was tall and courtly. His head was magnificent, made more so by a long, flowing white beard. He visited his patients in a buggy, meticulously kept, drawn by a horse as well known as himself. I recognized the sound of its wheels and the clop-clop of his horse's hoofs apart from all other vehicular combinations — or at least I thought I could — because often they awakened me in the night. This was so by reason of my grandmother's concept that good citizenship required her to help the indigent ailing, and Dr. Jepson's reliance on her unfailing willingness to demonstrate it by attending at any distance and at any time his patients who were in need of their skills.

These were the country doctors of the time, a vanishing species. They made little money and cheerfully went unpaid for their services by patients of meager means. Despite the great subsequent advancement in medical expertise, and the financial aid to the ailing provided by Medicare and other aspects of the Welfare State, I think in their virtual disappearance the American people have lost more in social values than they have gained in the dubious, wasteful and confused benevolences of the paternalistic superstate.

To Horatio, who found the appearance of the Ghost "wondrous strange," Hamlet replied, "There are more things in heaven and earth than are dreamt of in your philosophy." The eternal truth of this is borne out every day in human experience everywhere, and in Glasgow we had our share of evidences of the supernatural. I recall three in particular.

The Edmunds family owned a piece of rock known as the "madstone." Small, flat and of a slightly reddish tinge, it did not differ in aspect from thousands of others found in the soil. But the Edmunds stone possessed the mysterious quality of averting hydrophobia when a person was bitten by a rabid dog. Why and how this was so was an unsolved mystery. But there were many to swear from personal experience that, if the stone were applied without great delay to a wound inflicted by a mad dog it healed normally and quickly. This firm con-

viction was sustained by the fact that hydrophobia
had positively attacked others to whom the stone
had not been available, not always, but often enough
to engender absolute confidence in its recondite vir-
tues.

Though the local doctors were not prepared to
accept the belief as scientifically demonstrable, they
were not prepared to repudiate it as entirely lacking
credibility. Hence in my boyhood the community's
faith in the Edmunds madstone was as strong as
that of the cripples who throw away their crutches
at Lourdes, or as the faith of Chinese surgeons in
acupuncture.

A second mystery was supplied by Princess, one
of our two matriarch St. Bernards. One of her appointed duties each day was to lead our cows to the
town pasture in the morning and bring them back
in the late afternoon. Time after time she performed
this office flawlessly. But one evening one of her
charges was missing. Perceiving this on arrival
home, without a word having been spoken to her,
she rushed back to the pasture, and, after inspecting
the premises by nose, she proceeded to the residence
of my Aunt Victoria. There she found the missing
cow and duly chivvied her back to the place where
she belonged.

Could Princess count? In which case, was she
only being absentminded when she first returned

her charges? Or was Princess responding to some arcane prompting in performing something wondrous strange? I don't know the answer. But I do know the tale is true.

The third instance of the existence of the strangenesses Hamlet cited to Horatio was the presence in our community of a seeress. She was a Negro, old and totally blind. But she had, among other gifts, the ability to locate lost articles. I recall that my grandmother, having lost a twenty-dollar bill, consulted the seeress and was told that the missing item would be found "between two pieces of paper." After a long search it was discovered between two pages of a book which my grandmother had laid aside while reading a week or two before. In the same inexplicable fashion missing pieces of jewelry and other valuables were located for their owners.

In the hope of being credited with at least some fragment of discretion, I shall leave these mysteries for others to try to solve.

I realize I have portrayed Glasgow and Barren County in my boyhood as a community on the slopes of Utopia, and so it was for me and my like-situated companions. But in retrospect I also realize that the corruptions inherent in human nature were suppurating there on the general scale of mundane behavior.

Beneath the roofs of the large, comfortable houses there doubtless was the going percentage of crime, misery of spirit, incest, drunkenness, cruel gossip, discrimination against and exploitation of the humble, lust and greed. The drunkenness I was aware of, since every Sunday morning the town hummed with accounts of the toll alcoholic excess had taken of life and property the night before. And on the one occasion when — hiding in an outhouse near the town jail — I watched a mob take from his cell a Negro accused of rape, I beheld the horrid spectacle of lynch law in action.

But these matters lay on the far fringes of my consciousness: to me the community at large was as I have described it.

Perhaps because I was seldom the victor in those fistfights which boys fall to in the course of their upgrowing, I developed a fascination for champions in the "manly art of self-defense," as the promoters of professional boxing describe it. From my early years I informed myself of developments in this "art," and could reel off the names of principals in bouts which ranged from the flyweight to the heavyweight divisions. Who won, and how, and in what round, were statistics ever at the tip of my tongue. And when in time I came to know personally some of the great champions of the ring, I felt for them the admiration of the crowd that makes public idols of actors, military heroes and those politicians imbued with what a recent cliché designates as "charisma."

My first recollection of a prizefight concerns one morning, when I was about five years old (1892). My grandfather was sitting on the porch, reading the *Courier-Journal* of Louisville. As he turned a page he suddenly said "what a pity."

"What's a pity, Grandpa?"

"Why, that upstart James J. Corbett has knocked out the great John L. Sullivan."

Many decades later I was listening one day, in the *World* office in New York, to the general manager, Florence D. White, on the subject of boxing. He told of a time, long after the fight with Corbett, when, as a young reporter, he was sent to interview the great John L. The old paladin of the ring was enthroned in his saloon and casting aspersions on all his successors. "How would you handle them?" White said he inquired, to which Sullivan replied, "With one hand." Then, White added, "Sullivan loosened his belt and his belly fell out."

But this anecdote was no longer disillusioning for me; long since I had transferred my allegiance to Robert (Ruby Bob) Fitzsimmons who in 1897 had taken the championship away from Corbett at Carson City, Nevada, with the famed punch to the solar plexus.

I "heard," or, more accurately, "read" the fight at

Carson City while it was proceeding. In those days, long before radio and television, the Western Union and the Postal Telegraph Company sent running accounts of such events on their wires, and, as the strips arrived, they were pasted on the windows. My father took me to town to join the crowd before the Western Union office that was raptly watching each tape as it was put on the glass. When a bulletin, "Knockout by Fitzsimmons," appeared, followed immediately by the detail of the solar plexus blow, my treble voice arose among the baritones and the basses in jubilation.

This early-acquired interest in professional boxing, unusually served by the fact that when I was working on the *World* and the *Times* in New York in the Nineteen Twenties and Thirties I became a friend of the great promoter Tex Rickard, led to personal acquaintances with the great ring fighters of three generations. Years before I had made a pilgrimage to Bensonhurst, Long Island, where Fitzsimmons was living in retirement, and sat spellbound while he reminisced, in his strong Australian "strine," on his ancient battles. With Corbett at Carson City. With James J. Jeffries, when he lost the heavyweight championship. With Kid McCoy, the most brilliant — and most dubiously sportsmanlike — master of ring strategy. With Peter Maher, of whom Fitzsimmons had said to reporters before the bell: "There will be only two blows — one when I hit Maher and the other when Maher hits the floor." And it was so.

In New York I knew Corbett slightly. By that time "Gentleman Jim" had long since lost the championship to Jeffries and was earning a good living as an actor, an excellent one. Once he was describing his experiences when, as was then the custom of champions between fights, he was traveling with a road-show burlesque troupe. His contribution to the box-office draw of the show was to offer to box two one-minute rounds with anyone in the audience and present the challenger with one hundred dollars if he lasted the route.

"I remember it was in Cincinnati," said Corbett, "and at the time the manager announced the proposition I was most heavily hung over. Up from the audience came a big, muscular boy, much bigger than I, assistant to a local butcher as I learned afterward. His cheeks were rosy, his eyes were bright. I thought to myself, 'My God, suppose this kid (whom I could barely see) knocks out the heavyweight champion of the world.'

"But I knew something he didn't. I knew he was scared of me, but he didn't know I was scared of him. So after we came together and shook gloves, I tottered toward him and gave him a playful tap on the shoulder. Thinking it was the right thing to do, he tapped me back. The audience booed, the kid turned his head in surprise. I had one punch in my system. I let him have it, and he dropped. If he had got a punch in first, I fear that audience would have seen the heavyweight champion asleep on the floor."

Among the other masters of boxing with whom I became acquainted were Paul Berlenbach, Tommy Laughran and Jimmy Slattery, all light heavyweight champions; Jack and Tom Sharkey (the former of whom barely missed knocking out Jack Dempsey), McCoy, Mickey Walker, long king of the middleweights; Joe Jeannette, the great Negro fighter; Marvin Hart; Packy McFarland; Joe Choyinski, the skinny, stouthearted near-nemesis of Corbett; and both Dempsey and Gene Tunney. Thomas Hitchcock, the greatest polo player of this century, once invited me to dine at the Links Club in New York, where his guests of honor were Dempsey and Tunney, and their comments on their two contests for the heavyweight championship made the evening memorable because of the respect and friendship they showed to each other.

I grew to know Tunney quite well, to the point where we arranged that he extend his acquaintance from managers, trainers and boxers by dining with some of the many prominent New York men who had expressed a wish to meet him. Accordingly one evening, with my close friend J. Cheever Cowdin,

the seven-goal polo player on the Milburn and Hitchcock teams as co-host, I invited a group of these men
to meet the champion. He was the first professional
prizefighter most of them had met, and all were impressed with him as an individual. He spoke well and
familiarly of matters of general interest, including
their own, and certainly he was the handsomest man
among them.

After dinner all but two of the group gathered in
another room for cigars and brandy, the two being
Tunney and George Gordon Moore, a magnate in
the rapid transit industry, renowned as a polo player
and for his erudition. When half an hour had passed
with the pair still at the table, Cowdin urged me to
"break it up," saying that all the other guests wanted
to talk with Tunney. As I approached the table I
heard, with no particular surprise, Tunney saying:
"But, Mr. Moore, if Gibbon was not an enemy of
the Catholic Church, why, on page so-and-so, Volume X, did he write . . . ?"

Later Moore said to me: "Was that really Tunney,
the heavyweight champion of the world? One of
these nights somebody is going to knock him out
with a book!"

Another champion, a lightweight, I admired was
Ruby Goldstein, now a referee of professional boxing. For several months the senior Allan A. Ryan
and I followed him from one fight club to another

as he mowed down his victims in short order. Then came a night when he was booked at Coney Island in a match with a clumsy Nebraska farm boy named Ace Hudgkins. Ruby played with his opponent for a couple of rounds and, believing that the usual knock-out was closely impending, Ryan and I — and Cowdin who was with us — looked exultantly at one another. There was a sudden roar from the crowd, and we three turned to see our hero flat on his back.

I began this aficionado chronicle with Sullivan and Corbett in the Nineties. I end it with Dempsey, A. Charles Schwartz and Harry Greb.

Charlie Schwartz, of Wall Street, was a fairly good amateur boxer, his diversion from the hectic atmosphere of the Exchange. So when, at Saratoga one summer, a project for charity was undertaken, the idea entered the nimble brain of Herbert Bayard Swope that an exhibition match between Schwartz, a light heavyweight, and Dempsey could draw a large and most generous audience. Both were agreeable. There were to be two one-minute rounds. Throughout the first Schwartz was blasting the air with punches aimed at (but missing) Dempsey, which the latter never tried to return in kind.

Yet when the bell rang for the second round, Schwartz, after vainly trying to raise his arms, did not rise from his corner, I asked Dempsey why. "Well, you see," he said, "we have a trick in professional boxing: you just lean on the other guy's fore-arms, if you can, until you have worn him down. I just leaned on Charlie's forearms."

Harry Greb had an unconquerable fighting heart. He also was a good boxer with a potential knockout blow in each hand. With this equipment he had won the light heavyweight championship of the world, and in fifteen rounds had outpointed his most formidable challenger, Gene Tunney. But Tunney, much improved in skill and with more poundage, overcame Greb to win a return match which left indelible marks on both. On Tunney, because to win he was obliged to punish Greb severely, and this has distressed him ever since. On Greb, because the punishment he took was irreparable.

It was after this second fight that Tunney left the light heavyweight to join the heavyweight division, from which he eventually retired as unbeaten champion.

Out of the ring Greb was a modest and gentle creature. I can testify to this because, with my friend Philip Boyer, Greb and I often spent the late hours together in Jimmy Kelley's speakeasy in Greenwich Village, in the blighted years of national prohibition.

At the end of these evenings we were always joined by Boyer's favorite chauffeur, who at the time was running a taxicab business in Jersey City but came over to New York to see after Boyer whenever

Boyer was having a night on the town. The deference this big black man showed to Greb and Greb showed to him were affecting and fitting testimonials to the greatness each had displayed in the ring.

The Jersey City taxicab company owner was Joe Jeannette.

CHAPTER TEN

T HE THOUGHTS OF YOUTH are long, long thoughts," noted Mr. Longfellow, with the sound reservation that "a boy's will is the wind's will." In both respects I qualified. As I dreamed introspectively over the pages of the standard novelists and historians to whose works my grandfather's library was largely devoted, I conjured up myself successively as a successor to D'Artagnan, Charles James Fox, Montrose, Marmion, Ivanhoe, William Dobbin, Sydney Carton, Blackstone, David Copperfield, Mark Hopkins of Williams College, the Poe brothers of Princeton, Robert Fitzsimmons, Leibnitz (because he stood on the summit of omnium knowledge), Midshipman Easy, the Boy on the Burning Deck and many others whose lives, real or imaginary, had captured my fancy.

But as the realities in which life must be lived bore in on me more and more, at the expense of my visions, ambitions settled down, and I decided to become a professor of American history or a lawyer.

By the time I matriculated at Princeton in the autumn of 1904 I had decided I lacked the studious temperament and intellectual equipment for teaching. And the family financial assets having declined to the point where I had to maintain myself, the only way to do this was to get a paying job. This automatically terminated my idea of going on from college to law school — I had neither the years to devote to it nor the fortitude of character to attend classes at night after the long working days customary in that period.

At school and college I had written several papers which suggested to professors of English that I might have a talent for good observation of the kind essential to newspaper reporting, and even a clear and literate narrative style. On the basis of this opinion, plus an interest in the news of events which arose from their constant discussion in the family, I decided to try to get a job on a newspaper. But the problem was, how to elude a certain requirement of city editors of daily papers in those days: an applicant for payroll status must come to them with some field experience or train for six months without pay.

For a number of reasons Louisville was my only choice to begin a newspaper career. It is the metropolis of my home Commonwealth, Kentucky, in which the natives feel inordinate pride. Its great journalistic figure, Henry Watterson, was then an idol in every Kentucky family, including mine; his editorials had been read to me before I could read; and the *Courier-Journal* was our bible of current events. But, since I had to pretend previous experience, and the managing editor, Graham Vreeland — a family acquaintance — would know I had none, this was a foredoomed venture. Also, it was hardly likely that the managing editor of the *Louisville Times*, also owned by the Courier-Journal Company, would not learn of this if I represented otherwise.

Accordingly, I carried my deceit to the city editor of the *Herald*, a paper which, though ever on the brink of bankruptcy, was a lively shop, whose brilliant managing editor and page one columnist, A. T. Macdonald, daily stuck enough thorns in the majestic seat of the *Courier-Journal* to annoy it, if not to weaken its domination of the morning field.

When I asked the *Herald* for a job I had just spent fifty cents of my small capital for a night's lodging, and I was obliged to get on a payroll as quickly as possible. My remaining four dollars and fifty cents I expended in a round trip by train to my grandmother's house in Glasgow where I could count on free food and lodging while awaiting the decision of the *Herald* whether to employ the experienced reporter I vowed myself to be.

Two weeks later I got a telegram offering me a reporter's job at fifteen dollars a week. And it was not until I failed the intricate assignment of covering a big fire — a fundamental test of reportorial expertise — that my deception was unveiled. But I had shown enough promise to induce the *Herald* to keep me on.

The *Herald* occupied a crumbling building on Market Street, near Fifth. There were no elevators to the third floor where the news and composing departments adjoined — the business office was on the first floor, and the basement was given over to the creaking old presses, which were the best the poverty-stricken establishment could afford. Like every other city room of the period with which I was familiar — even those of the prosperous *Courier-Journal* and *Times* — the place was musty and strewn with the trash of reportorial activity.

But none of its inhabitants was concerned by these attendant circumstances of their labors. If any of us, including Mr. Macdonald (who actually had a cubicle of an office) had been taken forward in time to the swept and gleaming suites in which reporters work today, he would have thought he was in the throes of a particularly bad hangover.

I was assigned to a battered old desk on which stood a battered old typewriter, and, though I knew how to manipulate the latter mechanically, I did not know that the first page of newspaper "copy" must be surmounted by a "slug." This consists of the name (in small letters) of the producing reporter and a line giving the subject of the story: for examples, "Fourth Street Murder," "Wreck on the Daisy" (a trolley connecting Louisville with New Albany, Indiana, across the Ohio).

The preservation of my masquerade also required that I should "act" like a reporter. So I bent my ear to the slang of the trade, such as knowing what the city editor meant when he ordered me to write my story in "takes," if it was lengthy and the "deadline" was near, and even what a deadline was. I tossed my jacket onto a peg, whether or not the room was cold, cast the ashes from my four-cent cigar — El Toro by name — into the nearest of a battery of spittoons, and depreciated the fame of the star reporter with the others whom envy prompted to asperse his right to this eminence.

A common jest among itinerant reporters in that first decade of the twentieth century, when discussing other newsrooms, was that the pace at the *New Orleans Times-Picayune* was so leisurely, the only noise to be heard was the crackling of the logs in the fireplace, and that the reporters and editors wrote in longhand by candlelight. But, actually, on the *Herald*, the clacking of the linotype machines in the next room, added to the noise of our typewriters and loud conversational exchanges, conditioned us for writing in the most distracting circumstances — an ability whose value under the pressure of a developing event cannot be overemphasized. Bare and dusty illuminating bulbs, mostly hanging from the ceiling, suffused the quarters with a fishbelly light such as invests the paintings of El Greco. And in the long spells of stewing weather, typical of the climate of most riverine American cities, the feebly revolving fans served only to incandesce the hot gusts that came in through the open windows.

Old men forget, said King Harry at Agincourt, but old men also are prone to believe that stouter spirits emerge from hardships and discomforts in early working life than amid such luxuries as air conditioning, fluorescent lights, wall-to-wall carpeting, contour chairs and electric typewriters. Whatever the soundness of this postulate, I am glad I learned my trade in harsher working circumstances. Long hours, with only one day off a week — and the absence of union-enforced equality of earnings, regardless of superior talent, industry and character — produced, in my judgment, a self-discipline and professional devotion that is in shorter supply in journalism today.

Like many young reporters, especially those who had high marks at school in English composition, I burned with the ambition to invest my news stories with the "literary" touch. It is the most juvenile of delusions, for not only are news reporting and literature wholly different vehicles of written expression: they are mutually destructive to their objectives. Because I had the good fortune to begin work under editors who made this clear to me, I recovered rapidly from the fever. But while it possessed me I had it bad.

The first stage of my convalescence was marked by a strange and unexpected sensation. As I typed I began to laugh at the obscure words and recondite phrases I had selected to give literary quality to my product, and no cure of posturing is more effective than self-laughter.

I remember pouncing on a word I at first found delicious, intending to weave it into a profile of a citizen who exercised great power in the affairs of the State. The word was "puissant." But when I spoke it out loud it sounded convulsingly funny. And so (in order) did "pusillanimous," "hebetate" (that most stupid synonym for "dull"), and such phrases as "the scene beggared description," "a somber hush descended" — fancy frillings of rhetoric that I toyed with in my brief attempt to be literary and reportorial at the same time.

By this experience I realized, and for keeps, that the unadorned word and phrase, with restraint on adjectives, and only those fitly chosen, are the pure stuff of informative, honest, readable and — yes — distinctive journalism. And that, if a reporter wants to be a novelist, a poet, a dramatist, a philosopher or whatever, he must do it on his own time or damage both commodities.

Before the pretense of previous reportorial experience was shattered by my poor performance in carrying out the assignment to cover a big fire, the foreman of the composing room of the *Herald* could have exposed me. Suspecting how raw an amateur I really was, he had easily proved it a few days after I went to work by a practical joke which was standard practice among newspaper linotype operators when a new boy was taken on in the city room. This consisted of asking the recruit if he wanted to have a look at "type-lice," and, when the innocent had bent closely over a form to observe these reputed creatures, jamming the type together and inundating his face with a spray of inky water.

But, having had his joke to the great delight of the watching printers, the foreman and his crew magnanimously forbore to relay the story to the newsroom. Had they done so I might instantly have been reduced to my true status as an unpaid "cub," posing a problem of financial survival for which at the time I had no immediate solution.

The incident illustrates the fraternal relations between compositors and reporters that, at least in my experience, does not now exist with respect to the pressmen, stereotypers and the personnel of the business office. Perhaps this is because newsmen and printers consider their callings to be a sort of art not shared with the other departments. At any rate, on the *Herald*, and later when I was editorial manager of the *Courier-Journal* and the *Louisville Times*, this harmony was a firm condition. And of all my associates, in more than half a century of activity in newspapering, I had none more helpful in the newsroom, or more enjoyable in the saloons to which we repaired in common, than the mechanical workers and their foremen.

The foremen were good editors, too, and to them news and editorial staffs have owed a debt for many terrible goofs averted, and for miracles in overtaking closed forms, on the way to the stereotypers, so that vital corrections and additions could be made before publication. And Frank Jackson, the foreman of the composing room of the *Louisville Times*, had a talent which not only was unique, but inflicted an ever-living wound in the *amour propre* of the haughty sister paper, the *Courier-Journal*. For Jackson alone could, with total accuracy, decipher the scrawl which was the handwriting of the *Courier-Journal*'s celebrated editor, Henry Watterson.

Watterson, before he was thirty, had become so outstanding in American journalism and politics that the Associated Press distributed his national and international editorials to all its clients throughout the nation and abroad. Together with Henry T. Grady, of the *Atlanta Constitution*, Watterson led the movement to "bury the bloody flag" of the War Between the States.

He was either the keynoter or chairman of the Resolutions Committee of several Democratic National Conventions. He led in the formulation of the traditional party policy which he phrased as "tariff for revenue only." As an orator and lecturer he was in greater demand than nearly all his contemporaries. The conclusion of his lecture on Lincoln, for example, thrilled audiences in all parts of the country:

Born as lowly as the Son of God, in a hovel; reared in penury, squalor, with no gleam of light or fair surrounding; without graces, actual or acquired; without name or fame or official training; it was reserved for this strange being, late in life, to be snatched from obscurity, raised to supreme command at a supreme moment, and intrusted with the destiny of a nation.

The great leaders of his party, the most experienced and accomplished public men of the day, were made to stand aside; were sent to the rear, while this fantastic figure was led by unseen hands to the front and given the reins of power. It is immaterial whether we were for him, or against him; wholly immaterial. That, during four years, carrying with them such a weight of responsibility as the world never witnessed before, he filled the vast space allotted him in the eyes and actions of mankind, is to say that he was inspired of God, for nowhere else could he have acquired the wisdom and the virtue.

Where did Shakespeare get his genius? Where did Mozart get his music? Whose hand smote the lyre of the Scottish ploughman, and stayed the life of the German priest? God, God, and God alone; and as surely as these were raised up by God, inspired by God, was Abraham Lincoln; and a thousand years hence, no drama, no tragedy, no epic poem will be filled with greater wonder, or be followed by mankind with deeper feeling than that which tells the story of his life and death.*

Watterson's countenance — with its one blazing blue eye (he had lost the other in youth), its jutting jaw, its martial white mustache and goatee — badges of the old Confederates — was a constant lure to cartoonists for over fifty years. The fact that he preferred beer, champagne and brandy to the bourbon whiskey of his homeland was a news story whenever rediscovered, as often it was, by the metropolitan press. And, though the legend also had it that Watterson lunched on mint juleps at the Pendennis Club, his actual noonday habit was to repair

* Henry Watterson, *The Compromises of Life, and Other Lectures and Addresses, Including Some Observations on Certain Downward Tendencies of Modern Society* (New York: Fox, Duffield & Co., 1903), pp. 179–180.

to the backroom of a saloon near the *Courier-Journal* for a fare of chili and beer.

Among his diversions was poker, and each Saturday night for many years he joined an equally disposed group at the Louisville Hotel on Main Street. Since he rarely remembered to carry any cash, he would stop by the business office on the ground floor of the *Courier-Journal* and extract from the till a sum he considered sufficient to defray any losses he might sustain.

"Mr. Watterson" he called himself; it disgusted him when his surname was prefixed by "Colonel." But he enjoyed being referred to as "Marse Henry," which invariably he was in the political community, in cartoons, editorials, personal approaches and around the newspaper offices, including his own, and he so entitled his autobiography.

In figure he was of middle height and stocky. His walk was a quickstep; his voice was somewhat on the high side. Six days a week he rode the interurban trolley from "Mansfield," his home outside the town in Jefferson County, to the office and back. On the way in he read his copy of the *Courier-Journal* and made notes on what pleased or displeased him, or gave him an idea for an editorial. In the office he did no more than glance at the *Herald*. On his way out he read the *Louisville Times* and its competitor, the

Evening Post, taking little time for these with the usual remark that " a short horse is soon curried."

I did not meet Mr. Watterson, or even see him, until the summer of 1910, after I had become the Washington correspondent of the *Louisville Times*. Some field reports I had written, of the political situation in several states prior to the elections that foreshadowed the fatal Republican party split in 1912, had attracted his attention. He summoned me to the Presence, and the upshot was that I was appointed to represent the *Courier-Journal* in Washington also and instructed to report the 1910 campaign in the Haldeman paper of more general circulation.

I found the famous editor, for all his reputation as a fire-eater of politicians and devastator of whatever professional conceit his reporters had — he always referred to them as "the long-legged boys in the city editor's room" — a man of extreme consideration and civility. In time we became intimate friends. I was his companion in his hours of leisure, including those spent with the Watterson family at "Mansfield" and annual visits to New York for evenings of revelry at the Manhattan Club, the Lambs and the Lotus.

In the first he mingled with Tammany politicians; in the third with artists, professors and authors. But above these he enjoyed the Lambs because for most of his life Watterson was a patron and familiar of the stage, being something of an actor himself. Among his cronies were Nat Goodwin, Maurice Barrymore and John Drew.

In Louisville he was responsible for the early encouragement of the talent he discerned in a local girl, Mary Anderson, who in turn became the first lady of the American stage. And the reason Macauley's Theatre presented in Louisville the finest plays of every season as long as John Macauley, proprietor of the theater, and Watterson were alive was that Marse Henry used his influence to that end with the Louisville-born Mark Klaw and other moguls of Broadway.

Years later, on one of the occasions when I was in New York with Watterson, we attended a revival of Sardou's drama *Diplomacy*, in which William Gillette and Marie Doro played the leading roles. We had dined well at the Café Lafayette — I recall marveling at Watterson's consumption of a goblet of yellow Chartreuse — and my distinguished companion drowsed through most of the three acts. As each curtain fell, however, he sat up brightly and made a comment on the performance as follows:

Act One. Of course, this is nothing like as well done as when Georgie Drew and Maurice Barrymore were the stars.

Act Two. This is certainly better done than when

Georgie Drew and Maurice Barrymore were the stars.

Act Three. Of course, this is nothing like as well done as when Georgie Drew and Maurice Barrymore were the stars.

As the last curtain fell, Watterson announced we would visit "William" in his dressing room. My speculation as to what he would say was soon resolved. "William," he exclaimed, clapping Gillette on the shoulder, "of course this is a much better performance than when Georgie Drew and Maurice Barrymore played the leads."

His extraordinary energy having been fully restored by his naps, Watterson proposed we end the evening by supping at Mouquin's, and we did. Perhaps I should have asked his final choice between the two judgments he had alternately stated. But I didn't, and so I shall never know.

Chapter Eleven

ONE DIVIDEND OF WORKING on the *Herald* was its proximity to inexpensive places of refreshment that nevertheless were of the high quality which characterized most Louisville restaurants and saloons in those days. This proximity made possible merely a short absence from one's office when throat or stomach called for instant succor. Less than fifty yards of pavement separated the *Herald* from Sullivan & Brach's, as pleasant a saloon-restaurant as it has been my privilege to frequent — including 21 West Fifty-second Street, Moriarty's and Cavanagh's in New York.

Each afternoon, precisely at four o'clock, exquisitely baked Kentucky hams — I am of the school that holds them superior to Virginia's — were loaded onto a table across from the bar, and fifteen cents bought not only all the ham a patron desired to eat, but a shot glass of Spring Hill, one of the noblest straight bourbons that ever was distilled in a state where nobility is the minimum for whiskey. And there a fledgling reporter met and came to know certain leaders of the city and the Commonwealth whom otherwise he might never have encountered.

East of the *Herald* office, on Fourth Street, was the elegant tobacco emporium of Humler & Nolan where, although there was a line of the finest Havanas, impecunious smokers such as I could, without a hint of patronage, buy cheaper brands, including the aforementioned four-cent El Toros. Excellent and inexpensive late-night meals for reporters on duty were served at the American Restaurant on the same block on Market Street; with the kindly proprietors of Alsatian nationality your credit was good for even long periods of financial embarrassment. And just around the corner on Fourth Street, if luck at a crap or poker game had provided temporary affluence, was the Vienna, with a cuisine worthy of its name, including kaffee-mitschlag, true Würzburger and Pilsener, and such wiener schnitzels as might win the approval of any chef along the Ringstrasse.

We had few things to boast about on the *Herald*, though we beat "the Old Lady of Green Street," the *Courier-Journal*, with some frequency on the local news run, and Mr. Macdonald's sharp column on local affairs was not matched by any comparable feature of the competition. But there is a sense of vocation in the staff of an underdog newspaper that, on the *Herald*, was almost a tangible thing. It was a happy day on the *Herald* when the lordly *Courier-Journal* was humbled by a *Herald* "beat," as an exclusive news story is styled in the trade, though to outsiders better known as a "scoop." And this happened enough times to dispel the sensitivity which accompanies the status of the poor relation. Also, *Herald* reporters, such as I, were encouraged by tales of *gaffes* by *Courier-Journal* editors that had happened before our time. One I remember as giving us extreme pleasure concerned a night telegraph editor on the other morning newspaper. His name was Beriah Griffin; he was described as resembling a stuffed owl in appearance and a rooster in pomposity.

It seems that on the night of January 2, 1905, just before closing time of the three A.M. edition, an Associated Press bulletin came to his desk that reported one of the great military events of modern times: the capture of Port Arthur by the Japanese. Griffin, who had put on his hat and risen to go home, spiked the bulletin with the comment: "To hell with Port Arthur." And only the readers of the *Herald* next morning knew of the event which, with the defeat of the Russian fleet in Tsushima Strait in May 1905, marked the collapse of Russia in the 1905–1906 war.

The city editor of the *Herald* was Ben S. Washer, who for looks might have competed with King David if Bathsheba had made that the criterion for the grant of her favors. On the model of Kipling's "Six Honest Serving Men," he patiently impressed on his crew that a proper news story, in the early paragraphs, must always give the What and Why and When and Where and How and Who.

This mandatory formula has been supplanted in some degree by that exercise of "advocacy reporting," which accepts slanting and other coloring of the news on the theory that straightforward reporting is for the *Dullsville Gazette*. And, in untalented hands, it is. But reporters like Frank O'Malley of Dana's *New York Sun*, Herbert Bayard Swope of the *World* and Edwin L. James of the *New York Times* did not pass without leaving a professional posterity. And its members could, if asked, show those who slant and color the news to achieve reflection of their personal prejudices and political doctrines, how to produce an accurate and absorbing story without neglect of the essential factors.

Representatives of the new journalism now frequently commit what are, and always will be, cardinal reportorial sins — applauding at press conferences some statement they approve, or putting questions to the person being interviewed in the vein of prosecuting attorneys; employing pejorative or laudatory personal terms (the "able" Mr. Roe, the "evasive" Mr. Doe, "admitted" as a description of what was merely a "concession" of the obvious, and so on).

Such acts and attitudes by reporters were inadmissible as a matter of course on the newspapers where I learned the trade.

These attitudes include the formula of recording a news event in terms of the reporter's view of its "social significance," etc. The inevitable consequence is that the news is slanted and the report factually unreliable. And in a period of history when journalism, both printed and electronic, is highly suspect for credibility, "advocacy reporting" puts both more deeply on the defensive. This distrust is intensified when an editorial columnist with clear commitment to a particular point of view turns reporter in a field of his editorial interest.

In newspapers in Louisville and elsewhere when I joined the trade there was plenty of distortion in playing up the welcome news and playing down the unwelcome; of pressures by big advertisers and favored politicians to omit certain details in a report; of favoritism to individuals; of biased headlines; and of denying readers the publication of sound grievances. But these were dictated from the offices of publishers and editors: the poisons were not administered by the source of the news, the reportorial staff.

And in those days, too, there was ever available the antidote of competition: the presence in the community of watchful rival newspapers. This presence served well as a restraint on practices which take unfair advantage of the guarantee of freedom of the press in the First Amendment — responsibility and honesty being assumed as the exchange for this guarantee.

Now, in far too many communities, newspaper readers no longer have the protection of this punitive rod of competition from the arrogance and bias that tend to develop in newspapers with a monopoly of their field. And in such situations, while the strength of monopoly is sufficient to reject pressures from big advertisers, these pressures in the period I am recording were rarely more than such requests as eliminating the name of a store in which occurred something that would be "bad for business." In terms of news manipulation they were insignificant when compared with the pressures of the present that have induced newspapers, in reports of crime, to omit details essential to identification of the criminal and to public awareness of the population groups from which crime is more likely to emerge. Thus in Washington, when the police ask for public assistance in apprehending rapists, burglars and murderers, the readers of one of its newspapers are usually denied knowledge of a vital factor in correctional and self-protective activity if the criminal is a Negro.

The newest member of the *Herald*'s reportorial staff, I was also the most curious. I watched my seniors at their work in a constant effort to discover which of their qualities had sufficiently impressed the city editor to entrust them with the most desirable areas of news production — general assignments and politics at the top of the list. After a while I decided that, though industriousness, personality and the art of striking presentation of the news were indispensable in attaining senior status, these reporters had three intangible assets without which their product would have been routine: knowing the right questions and the right people to ask them of, and having a "nose for news." Since the latter is congenital and an instinct, a reporter has it or he hasn't.

Charles Moore, a fellow reporter, had all three qualifications. Though seemingly he was indolent, bored, indifferent and cynical where the collection of news was concerned, the stories he pecked out on his typewriter were always literate, authoritative, comprehensive and well organized. Yet, knowing the deadline for turning in his reports was fast approaching, Moore would spend a while writing doggerel before beginning with breakneck speed to type his story. Two of these verses I remember well.

The trial of Harry Thaw for the murder of Stanford White was dominating the news, and, in a pioneer use of psychology by the defense, a certain Dr. Wiley had testified that Thaw was not guilty of deliberate murder because he was afflicted by an errant "pneumogastric nerve." As I craned my neck, Moore was typing the following, the beginning a parody of a famous poem by Robert Browning:

> Beautiful Evelyn Thaw is sad,
> Come and sit by her side an hour.
> There is her mother — she has no dad —
> There sits Harry, glum and sour,
> Dr. Wiley has left the stand,
> Maybe 'twere best he had stayed away.
> But, speaking of pneumogastric nerves,
> Well, say, the Doc was sure okay.

Another time, when Czarist Russia was alarming the British by what seemed reactivation of a long hunger to occupy India, I saw Moore risking his deadline with this play on Kipling:

> Hatless, coatless, toothless,
> Cadging a drink at the bar,
> Me Uncle Mike the Fenian
> Is telling them near and far,
> Over and over the story,
> "Beware of the Great Flim-Flam;
> "There is no truce with Gazebo,
> "The lion that looks like a lamb."

The star *Herald* reporter was considered to be Gus Crain, a status verified by the fact that his beat was "General Assignments." This meant he normally was chosen to cover the big story of the day, and though by-lines were rare on the *Herald* and non-existent on the *Courier-Journal*, he would be assured of them — a privilege from which local fame and access to ordinarily closed sources inevitably accrued.

Crain, a gangling youth, tireless of leg, and possessed of a nose which detected news where others would miss it, made the most of all these gifts of fortune. His excess of imagination and tendency toward purple prose sometimes put the *Herald* on the defensive, but on the whole Crain could have competed with reasonable success with the best reporters anywhere. (Eventually he established in Chicago *Advertising Age*, a topflight journal of that turbulent trade.) Envying and admiring him simultaneously, I decided my ambition: I would get the post of "General Assignments" somewhere, and attain the extravagant height of a salary of five thousand dollars a year.

Our chief political reporter was George Henry Sussex Peters, a small and wiry man whose resemblance to Sir John Tenniel's depiction of the Mad Hatter in *Alice* was completed by the fact that his hat, too, was jammed to his temples. English by parentage, Peters also retained strong traces of that London accent known as "cockney," though wherever he was born, I do not believe it was within the sound of Bow Bells. This is because I, full of Dickens and

Thackeray, could stump him anytime on what was where in London.

But the bulldog strain was in him, and it showed in his pursuit of politicians with news they were not anxious to impart and he was determined they should. The *Herald*'s coverage of politics did not match that of the *Courier-Journal* generally, but Peters operated selectively, and within those limits he competed well. Each time he returned with a good story from the City Hall, the Jefferson County Courthouse, the legislature at Frankfort, outstate where something politically delicious was going on, a revised ambition mounted in my breast: someday I would be a five-thousand-dollar-a-year political reporter.

In the *Herald*'s tiny complex of subeditors — "editor" was a title good for swaggering a bit around town — there was a delightful character whose field was general news of Kentucky communities outside the metropolis. His name was Sam Severance (it brought to my mind Dick Swiveller in *The Old Curiosity Shop*), and his kindness and helpfulness to this raw beginner abide in my memory. Severance was also a droll teller of country yarns, the drollness enchanced by wonderful grimaces on a face seamed, though young, with networks of wrinkles.

His birthplace was in Lincoln County, at Crab

Orchard, where Colonel William Whitley had built the first house of other than wooden construction (it was brick which had been carried over the mountains to what was then Virginian Transylvania); and, as a Kentucky history buff, I deeply savored this natal distinction. While state editor — before moving to assistant city editor — Severance's job was to watch the weeklies, biweeklies and few dailies outside Louisville for stories or for leads of what could be developed as stories. This (I later discovered when I succeeded to the job) involved a great deal of rewriting from the sources, as often without credit as could safely be managed, a wide acquaintance with country and town editors, attendance on meetings of the state press association (that is, when the *Herald* was willing to spare the money), and a recruitment of county colleagues in the event statewide news had broken outside Louisville and competition required that the *Herald* have a direct report by wire, for which the local received the magnificent stipend of five dollars. Coverage of news of the interior by dispatching a member of the staff to the scene was almost an emergency measure because of the permanent poverty in which the paper was obliged to operate.

The owner at the time of my initiation was George A. Newman, Jr., son of probably the most adventurous druggist who ever supplied grist for the pestle. The elder Newman, wanting George to have a glamorous and important career, had bought the *Herald* for his son from the profits of a patent medicine, "California Syrup of Figs," which he had compounded. And throughout a number of years young George gallantly competed with the prosperous *Courier-Journal*, a shoestring in a market where the rival could offer custom-made boots.

My first assignment was on a Sunday when, news being light, both industry and luck were needed to produce a story. With a commission to roam my reportorial area, the East End, I learned at a police station that two officers had just gone on a rescue mission to the riverfront, at the foot of Brook Street. I followed to find them leaning over a man of middle age who was lying, obviously ill, on the beach. The officers had called an ambulance but before it arrived I got my story. I hurried back to the office and pounded out a tearjerker indeed.

The story, which appeared on page one of the *Herald* Monday, July 9, 1906, is here reprinted with all its infirmities of hyperbole and professional inexperience because to it, after my claim to have come to the *Herald* as an experienced reporter was shattered some months later, I owed the decision of the City Editor to keep me on the payroll anyhow.

BROKEN BY SORROW AND ILL HEALTH REAL
HERO IS FOUND BY POLICEMEN ON RIVERFRONT

———————

Still Clutching Evidence of His Heroism in Saving
Train as His Most Precious Possession, He Tells a Sad
Story of Misfortune and Grief.

———————

"The bearer, Mr. Harmon, flagged No. 709 at
trestle 708, the trestle being damaged.
          'O. H. Woofter, Conductor, B. and O. R.R.' "

Clutching this statement written on a telegraph blank
in a scrawling hand, evidence of his heroism and his
most precious possession, Frank Harmon was found lying outside a shanty at the foot of Brook Street yester-
day afternoon, bearing in his tremendous build and
stoicism under sorrow and sickness the earmarks of a
real hero.

Two boys found him, and informed officers Barrett
and Wagner.

When the officers arrived they saw a roughly dressed
man of superb proportions curled along a plank, his
head pillowed upon a rusty shovel, and moaning faintly.
His first words dispelled any idea of his intoxication that
the officers might have held, and they saw immediately
that he was very ill. His name is Frank Harmon, fifty-
three years of age, and he had worked his way down to
Louisville on the packet from Aurora, Indiana. He had

been a prosperous teamster of Pittsburg, and had buried his wife and four children as a consequence of typhoid fever. The necessarily heavy doctor bills had exhausted his little store, and, sick of the old and sorrow-charged associations of his deserted home, he secured service on the boat bound for Louisville to begin anew.

Constant attendance at the sickbeds of his family had made his habits of eating and sleeping irregular and he had worked all Saturday night in a pouring rain, unable to eat anything, friendless. When he reached Louisville this morning his stomach pains became acute. He laid [sic] down in the diminutive shelter of the shanty, expecting soon to be able to resume his way uptown. He became worse, and he had been lying there in agony and helplessness for four hours when the officers arrived. They immediately summoned the ambulance, and, whispering his thanks, Harmon entered and was taken to the city hospital.

Before he was supported into the vehicle, he handed the foregoing telegram, his most precious possession, to the *Herald* reporter.

Harmon in health must have had the very proportions of the hero the above telegram tacitly declares him. He is over six feet tall, and weighed 216 pounds of muscle and bone before his sorrows.

Among the other members of the *Herald*'s news-staff was a tall, kindly Canadian whom Mr. Macdonald, his fellow countryman, had imported, and who was to be the unintentional cause of my voluntary separation from the paper. His name was S. J. Duncan-Clark; he had a wife and a young daughter to whom, along with the generous hospitality of his home, I owed frequent breaks in the solitude of a young reporter with an income of fifteen dollars a week. (Chance decreed that, years later, as the Washington correspondent of the *New York Times*, I should employ his daughter, Mrs. Gay Tomlinson, in the Bureau's library.)

The depression of 1907 having compelled the *Herald* to cut its staff, I discovered that Duncan-Clark was included in the cut, irrespective of his abilities, because his salary was high according to *Herald* standards. In grateful remembrance of his kindness, and being myself without any family obligations, I volunteered for the bowstring in his place. My offer was accepted with an embarrassing lack of reluctance, and I found myself looking for a job again. The brevity of this condition of unemployment and what it led to will be dealt with later in this narrative.

But while on the *Herald* I had graduated to full incumbency of a "district police" beat. My duties were to report crimes (capital and otherwise), deaths, accidents and the like in the East End of town. These involved nightly checks with hospitals, undertakers, police and firefighting precincts, much of this in person instead of on the telephone — a pro-

cedure which would have been exhausting had the
No. 5 Engine Company not loaned me a horse from
time to time. And before setting out to cover my territory I spent several hours rewriting the obituaries
in the afternoon newspapers — the *Times* and the
Evening Post. In so doing I sought to verify everything stated as a fact, particularly the spelling of the
names of the departed and his survivors, and the
causes of death. After a few arduous weeks of check-
ing these details by personal visits to bereaved households all over town, I learned from veteran predeces-
sors that such efforts were far too conscientious as
well as too physically destructive, and thereafter
used the telephone.

In a certain context the word "old" is one of the
warmest in English, and nationals of other Western
countries have assured me that this is true of their
own languages when a person is addressed or introduced as an "old" friend. Such a one is the only colleague of my days on the *Herald* that I have never
lost touch with in the more than six decades that
have elapsed since we met.

Malcolm W. Bayley was a fresh-faced kid from
across the Ohio in Indiana when he was turned over
to me for training in the duties of a district police reporter, from which status I was about to graduate.
For a couple of weeks he accompanied me on my

rounds of the East End where I knew almost everyone and everything essential to getting the news
thereof. We found each other's company agreeable,
and the consequence was an abiding and rewarding
friendship. After numerous adventures in various
fields — the last in college education — Bayley returned to Louisville for some years, and to a regular
correspondence with me about the changes which
would make us both strangers, asking for direc-
tions, in the city we once so intimately knew.

At one period during his service for the *Herald*,
the pressure of economy even reached the point
where Bayley covered sports as a sideline effort after
his daily news stint was done. In view of the prime
circulation value of comprehensive reporting in this
field, the desperation of the *Herald* management at
the time could not be made more apparent than by
the low priority assigned to sports reporting.

The higher spheres to which I attained were, successively, the reporting of municipal affairs, news of
the law courts, and succession to Sam Severance as
state editor after his promotion to assistant city editor. On the legal and municipal affairs runs I came to
know judges, Commonwealth and defense attorneys,
the politicians who by definition are active in area of
the law, particularly the criminal, and the high police officers to whose patrolmen, corporals and ser-

geants my acquaintance on the East End beat had been confined. Also, I formed lifetime friendships with my rival court reporters from the *Courier-Journal* and *Times* and the *Evening Post* — Eustace Williams and Charles Neville Buck, Jr. Through them I learned of the system of exchanging carbon copies of routine news stories — an underground but abiding practice by which the toil of reporting is most agreeably diminished, though forbidden by self-interest when an important story can be captured as an "exclusive."

Charlie Buck fascinated me on several counts. He had written excellent novels of Kentucky mountain life. He was romantically and darkly handsome; and his father had been Minister to Peru (though known in the Foreign Service principally because, when President Cleveland saw his name on his appointment list, he growled: "Who in the hell is Buck?"). Moreover, Charlie was the certified rival of an actual du Pont for the hand of the beauteous Miss Moxham of Bullitt County, who lived on an estate on Salt River. He lost out to the du Pont, gallantly acknowledging the loss in a poem written in the manner of Swinburne:

I would rather see you married
To Thingum-Thingum-Thee [the du Pont]
Than see you come a-cropper
In the Big Countree [apparently, penury with Buck].

In the course of my municipal affairs assignment I had my first experience of being denounced publicly, accompanied by the threat of a suit for libel. It was to be many decades before the Supreme Court of the United States made successful libel actions by public figures virtually impossible, and in 1907 newspaper owners feared for their revenues when taken into court on this charge. I had written in a published news story that some colleagues suspected that a certain alderman, naming him, might have taken a bribe in exchange for a favorable vote. He was a burly citizen of Sudeten extraction, and his bellows for a retraction, and for my head on a platter, shook the beams of the aldermanic chamber.

The unexpectedly happy outcome was that the *Herald* refused to retract, hinted at producing supporting documents (which we didn't have), and limited reparations to an offer to print any statement the wounded behemoth furnished, provided it was sufficiently civil and not longer than the incident warranted. But the experience taught me a valuable professional lesson: don't print or circulate rumors that affect the reputation of an individual, however convinced of their authenticity, unless fortified by evidence — in which case they would not be just rumors.

I profited by this lesson twenty years later when I was editorial manager of the *Courier-Journal* and

Times. I had run a Sunday feature on the representation of an itinerant silhouette artist that we should have it exclusively, and, when it appeared simultaneously in the competition, I wrote a letter to managing editors throughout the country narrating the incident and naming the artist. He promptly sued for libel (or perhaps slander), but I had the goods on him, so testified, and the judge dismissed the action.

But I learned something else of value from my run-in with the furious alderman: there are ways in less grave situations to take a sly poke at a public person and yet stay within the reportorial sphere. I am indebted to Raymond P. Brandt for an example of this satisfying technique.

When Brandt was the Washington correspondent of the *St. Louis Post-Dispatch*, a reporter on his staff wrote, and Brandt forwarded to St. Louis, a story including this: "Rep. Dewey Short, the Ham Fish of the Ozarks . . ." The comparison was excised by the St. Louis editors before publication, on the ground that it was not reportorial, but an editorial comment instead, obliquely pinning the fault of excessive garrulity on the Representative from Dutchess County, New York. Brandt's young man was downcast. "I thought it was pretty funny," he said. "I'll show you how to get it in the paper," said Brandt. "Next time write 'Rep. Dewey Short, who *has been called* [italics supplied] the Ham Fish of

the Ozarks . . .' " And, since this was a fact (hadn't
the reporter just so called him?) the phrase duly appeared in the *Post-Dispatch*.

Soon after the East End of the city was made my
territorial domain as a police reporter, in which capacity I first plied my trade (Fourth Street marked
the boundary line where the West End began), I
met my rival, Alwin Seekamp of the *Courier-Journal*,
at No. 5 Engine Company's firehouse and was instantly beguiled by his courtly and welcoming manner. This dreamy state was abruptly shattered when
he promptly gave me a hard initiation. It was considered a good joke on greenhorns to work up an in-
teresting fictitious but harmless story with an ob-
liging nurse at the City Hospital, a doctor, or a cop
disposed, like Gilbert's Mikado, to innocent merriment.

I had been only a couple of days on the job when
I was smitten by the first page of the *Courier-
Journal:* it carried a story of a discovery on my
beat of a reputed argosy of family precious jewels —
giving the name of the fortunate heir. Upset as I was
by the first "scoop" against me I had encountered,
City Editor Washer was even more so, as he elo-
quently made plain to me. Happily, investigation
proved that the treasure was a small hoard of gold
coins — value less than one hundred dollars — found
by an East End druggist in an old trunk. I for-

get whether Brainerd Platt, the *Courier-Journal*'s dreaded City Editor, when the *Herald* printed the exposé I was instructed to write, visited on Seekamp any of the tortures he was credited with conceiving. But the incident fused a wary friendship between Seekamp and me.

In my progress to becoming a veteran in police reporting, Captain Andy Krakel, commander of the Headquarters precinct, was only one of several officers of the law who helped me through my apprenticeship. Four others who particularly come to mind were Captain James Hendricks, of the "Tenderloin" (whorehouse and gambling area), Lieutenant James Kinnarney, and Major Pat Ridge and Major Edward Burke, successively Night Chief of Police.

Hendricks was a handsome and daring officer whose scruples were no fewer than many other policemen at the time. He wore tailor-made uniforms, heavy with gold braid, and his badge was of gold, encrusted with diamonds. His waxed mustache was beautiful to behold, his physical courage was unlimited, and a reporter to whom he took a fancy was lucky indeed. While I was covering the East End he gave me many a good story. And when he retired, in great if somewhat mysterious prosperity, to open a saloon, I never suffered from the restrictions of the "dry" laws — a privilege which, at my request, he extended years afterward to the owner of the pro-dry

Courier-Journal and *Times* after they were sold by the Haldeman family and national prohibition darkened the land.

Captain Hendricks also was a fountain of realistic advice. I remember an occasion when, one of my colleagues showing signs of depression, the Captain counseled him to try a refresher course outside the marriage bed. Another instance of his kindly concern arose when the *Herald* cartoonist and I, having imbibed a trifle too much bourbon, and disliking the smell of eggs served to us in an all-night eatery, threw the said eggs at the door at the moment a policeman whom we did not like — and who didn't like us — was entering the café. He promptly arrested us and conveyed us to the small jail of City Hall. When we got news of this to Captain Hendricks, his indignation was terrible to behold. Did not the idiot cop realize we were the Captain's friends, and newspapermen to boot? In about three minutes our cell door flew open, and the offending cop only escaped suspension by our pleas to the Captain for mercy.

My fellow egg-thrower was a lad who attained national fame when his cartoons became syndicated. Among his immortal creations were the Terrible-Tempered Mr. Bang, the Toonerville Trolley (based on the meandering of the Brook Street trolley cars in Louisville), and the Powerful Katrinka. His name was Fontaine Fox (Fontaine is pronounced "Fountain" in Kentucky), and he lived to rejoice millions of newspaper readers with his gentle social satires.

Fox and I "ran around together," as the saying went. One noonday, as we were about to enter a saloon for the first custom-fixed shot of bourbon to strengthen us for the rigors of the day, we encountered a very pretty girl. She was carrying a cardboard suitcase and wore a facial expression so woebegone that we decided she needed help which we might be able to provide. Her tale was that she was a miner's daughter from Short Creek, West Virginia, from which she had run away to Louisville with a racetrack tout who had just deserted her and left her penniless. Did we by chance know where she could find a humble lodging and a job whose pay would provide her with even minimum sustenance?

Did we not? The consequence was that, in her comfortable room whose rent we paid from week to week until she proved to be virtuous to the point of ingratitude (Fox expressed the opinion that her underthings were made of iron), she gave a splendid imitation of the London trollop whose impregnability drove Casanova nigh onto crazy. Or of the Seville baggage whom Pierre Louÿs described in *La Femme et le Pantin*. So we learned about women from her.

Lieutenant Kinnarney eventually left the force to become chief of the special police at Churchill Downs and other racetracks. But while I knew this merry

Irishman he was a constant source of delight because of his informal methods of law enforcement. Witness: One morning, about three A.M., Captain Krakel and I were sitting outside Police Headquarters with Kinnarney. Suddenly he jumped from his chair, darted across Fifth Street and fired three shots at a vanishing, shadowy figure. Captain Krakel demanded furiously to know the reason. "Well," said the Lieutenant, "it was a Negro and he was acting suspicious." In the course of a lecture from Krakel that would have withered a less buoyant spirit, I remember this: "And another thing — how could you tell his color in the dark?"

I owe the Captain more grateful recollections. He took me one night to all the houses of pleasure on Green Street and its counterpart highways and introduced me to the madams and their girls. If I had any impulse to become a habitué in night-town, this tour extinguished it. And such was his purpose.

But because I was generally on late duty — my quitting time being four A.M. when I moved to the Associated Press — I was very well acquainted with these ladies of the evening in their time of relaxation. The only restaurant open at that hour was in their district, and its regular patrons included them and me. The girls were more often bovine than like unto gazelles, but the best of company for a lonely young man whose contacts with the human race were made mostly in the hours of darkness.

As the numerous readers throughout the nation of *A House Is Not a Home* can attest, the madam of such an establishment can be a citizen of great interest in communities far less sophisticated than New York City, where the author of the above-named book plied her trade. With respect to that trade, Louisville, at the time of which I write, was certainly not as sophisticated as New York or Chicago in these matters. Nevertheless, "Miss Ethel," as she was known, could have won a popularity contest over all others in her field of operation because she was gracious, very witty, handsome, refined in manner (but not to the point of being prissy), and very careful to provide no basis for even the suspicion that she had contributed to the delinquency of any of her girls.

She and I developed a pleasant acquaintanceship as a by-product of police reporting, and as fellow customers of the only restaurant where a good meal was available at the conclusion of each of our daily labors — four A.M. So it came about in 1907 that she invited me to take Christmas dinner with her and her flock in their luxuriously appointed residence, and I gratefully accepted.

I was so new in town that I had acquired no friendships among families from which Christmas dinner invitations came later. And a small spirit of adventure, heightened by dismissing thoughts of what my folks would think, led my willing feet toward the feast. It was a most agreeable and respectable occasion.

Miss Ethel was her kindly and entertaining self; and her charges behaved themselves like young ladies at a seminary tea. Finally, the menu was exquisite, and I thoroughly enjoyed myself — the more so because, when I boasted of this social success to colleagues, I was the envy of Newspaper Row.

I recall only dimly the table conversation except that no reference was made to the ancient profession of the members of the company. But I do remember with what grace and dignity Miss Ethel carved the Christmas fowl and presided over the board; that the girls ranged from the young and pretty to more worn and older types; that the gossip was polite and dealt with prominent patrons of the establishment, yet without identification by name; and that on my discovery that two of the girls were from my native area, I considered it a creditable average in a Commonwealth of one hundred and twenty counties. There certainly were cocktails served before dinner, and I suppose, in so high-grade a brothel, there was champagne during the feast. But, since Christmas was not an off-day for me, and I recall no trouble at the office, I assume I reported for duty as usual and in working condition.

The decor of Miss Ethel's house is more clearly imprinted on my memory because, as a police reporter, I called there several times in collecting some detail of a news story. The furniture of the parlor, including many mirrors, was an elegant mixture of several periods, mainly Victorian; the walls were hung with nude portraits, not all of them chaste, but none as pornographic as the postcards peddled around the Café de la Paix; the dining table and chairs were made of a dark, gleaming wood which may have been mahogany; and the napery and cutlery were spotless and gleaming.

Major Pat Ridge was an intellectual — rare on the police forces of those days. Brave, kind and just, he was an important force in helping me into maturity. And a very special bond between us was his love and knowledge of the songs, poems, novels and folk stories of the Irish, reflecting a culture which had beguiled me since I had in childhood devoured the works of Charles Lever and Tom Moore.

Major Edward Burke, the fifth in my quintet of special friends on the force, was a man of great and dignified presence and scholarly tastes who had great compassion toward the waifs and rebels of society he constantly dealt with as Night Chief. His faith was complete that the Catholic Church was the surest highway to eventual paradise for people of good will, and in the Pope as God's earthly surrogate. After I told him of the many times I had done the Stations of the Cross, in demonstration of my devotion to a Catholic girl with whose beauty and goodness I had once been smitten, he accepted me as a sort of understanding heathen theologian; we often spent the late hours discussing matters canonical and ritual. In consequence I was able to count on his generous assistance in helping me track down news which it was my responsibility to cover. I wish this excellent officer and man had lived to see that grandson, decades later, become one of the ablest members of the Foreign Service of the United States, with the rank of Ambassador.

There was a sixth friend in uniform, though not of the police, to whom I owed many delightful hours of companionship, lubricated with the nectar of Kentucky. These talks occurred aboard the United States Coast Guard vessel that was stationed on the Ohio River at the foot of Fourth Street — the only river-borne craft of this service in the country at the time. Its uniqueness arose from the fact that at Louisville the Ohio plunges in a series of rocky rapids that drop the level of the main stream by sixty feet. The Coast Guard vessel and its crew were constantly engaged in rescuing rivermen whose boats had been swept by the powerful "Indiana Chute" beyond the entrance to the canal that afforded safe traverse to rejoin the river beyond the falls.

Lieutenant John F. Gillooly was my friend's name, and, with the Celtic fancy and brogue which lent magic to his speech, he spun tales by the hour while I sat entranced. The accounts ranged from daring rescues of crews whose vessels had been drawn into the treacherous current — these often produced a good story for the paper — to exploits of early Irish warrior-kings and mischiefs wrought by the "little people," the leprechauns, with porkpie hats. Lieutenant Gillooly believed in their existence, or led me to think he did, and when long afterward I was in Ireland I found myself looking hopefully for them astride every blackthorn.

As my reportorial scope expanded from the police and court beats to local politics, to an occasional assignment to the state legislature in Frankfort and to watching the Night Riders at their tobacco-barn burnings, my qualifications for state editor expanded with it. My rise from the original fifteen dollars a week to eighteen dollars then mounted to twenty dollars, and I was on my way to the peak of my ambition — to close my newspaper career at a ripe and healthy old age, with an annual salary of five thousand dollars.

Throughout the Nineteen Thirties, and again in the late Sixties and early Seventies, college graduates entered upon their normal period of productive labor with very gloomy prospects. The newspapers recounted daily the statistics of their vain searches for gainful and otherwise promising employment. Young people highly trained in technology and the liberal arts could find few jobs suitable to their qualifications and were obliged to take the even fewer ones available that required only duties which the less educated could do as well. Ph.D.'s were a drug on the job market in the fields for which they were splendidly trained, even in education. And it was the common belief of the generation affected that the promise of the American system was more in default than ever before. But the period from the summer of 1906 to the autumn of 1907, when I was serving my novitiate as a newspaper reporter, was quite as bleak for the aspiring college-trained young American. The "Panic of 1907," foretold months before by the New York banker Jacob M. Schiff, was running its devastating course.*

The fact that the depression had taken hold of the economy came into general public consciousness on March 14, 1907, with the heavy fall of prices on the

* For the mention of Schiff's warning and some other details of the 1906–1907 depression I am indebted to Mark Sullivan's indispensable history titled *Our Times.*

New York Stock Exchange. On October 21 there was a run of depositors on the Knickerbocker Trust Company that forced the institution to suspend payments on October 22, with New York City police herding away the anxious throngs from its doors. And this situation was repeated all over the United States as bank after bank suspended payments.

The basic cause for the panic was the lack of a national banking system, but President Theodore Roosevelt blamed it on "ruthless businessmen hiding behind the breastworks of corporate organization" — those whom he also called "the malefactors of great wealth." How vigorously this attribution was disputed, together with the charge that T.R. was the real "panic-maker," is sufficiently indicated by the following blast in the *New York Sun:* "Hail Caesar. We who are about to bust salute thee!"

Employees, including us on the *Herald*, were paid in improvised currency (scrip) for a considerable period, which certain pawnbrokers allied with politics redeemed in cash at a ten per cent discount, but a much more unpleasant and apprehensive feeling it was when some merchants rejected scrip entirely. However, by reason of generous and constructive steps taken by some of the very Wall Street financiers whom the President was attacking as the cause of the condition, the currency crisis was abated before the end of 1907, though the business depression, as is its nature, continued for some time thereafter.

The hero of the currency relief was J. P. Morgan the First. Together with James Stillman, president of the National City Bank of New York, he met with many persons of great wealth and set up a rescue pool. Morgan and Stillman imported $100 million in gold from Europe; John D. Rockefeller, Sr., contributed $10 million in government bonds, free; Secretary of the Treasury Cortelyou offered $150 million of government money to national banks; and, though these seem small sums in this era of trillions of dollars, confidence in the currency was restored.

The text of President Roosevelt's State of the Union address to Congress, December 3, 1907, gave small indication of the panic which had just been experienced by the American people. Declaring that no sounder business conditions existed in any country than those in the United States, he merely urged the "foolish hoarders" of currency to return their money to the banks. Don't fear the extension of the Federal government in the form of a national banking act, he said; just observe how well the Pure Food and Drug Act, which had been long delayed by powerful opposition, was working.

The remainder of the address was as calm in tone: The United States must not depart from the principle of the protective tariff. The eight-hour-a-day law for workers must be greatly extended in its coverage. There should be many more vocational schools — mechanical in the cities, agricultural on the farms (partly because the family farm must be preserved as a vital element of the social economy). Labor-management disputes which paralyzed normal commerce must be made subject to "compulsory investigation" by Congress, followed by the grant of sufficient Federal power to deal firmly with such disputes. Army officers up to the rank of major should undergo rigid fitness tests, particularly of their horsemanship. The wisdom of United States military intervention in Cuba had been proved and soon a free election would restore peace and orderly government on the island. And, by the way, the fleet was on its way to the Pacific through the Straits of Magellan to show whom it may concern how completely the United States was able to defend itself.

Panic? What panic?

During the presidential campaign of 1908 I got my first taste, though a slight one, of reporting in a national framework. I was assigned to cover only a few of the appearances of the candidates, William H. Taft and William Jennings Bryan, two in the state outside Louisville. But I retain certain distinct remembrances of the presidential candidates and the meetings, and of a campaign orator who came to Louisville to speak in behalf of an obscure citizen named Thomas L. Hisgen, presidential candidate of the Independence Party — both candidate and party being this orator's personal property.

This interloper was William Randolph Hearst. To a packed audience in Phoenix Hill Auditorium he introduced a political trick unknown at the time to me and probably to all but the major party professionals who were present as a matter of curiosity. At one point in his oration Hearst was interrupted by what seemed to be a hostile heckler who cried, "You are talking through your *hat* there." To which came the instant riposte, in that high piping voice which contrasted so strangely with the driving force of its possessor: "I'm talking *to* a hat there!"

Not until an expert in such matters informed me that both the thrust and the riposte were the opposite of spontaneous did I learn of the stratagem of planted heckling. To cap my disillusionment, my informant showed me proof sufficient that the heckler was paid ten dollars for his performance.

(In the Nineteen Thirties, I met Hearst for the first time and he confirmed that the verbal exchange at Phoenix Hill had been arranged in advance. He was visiting William Randolph Hearst, Jr., who had become a friend of mine, at Sands Point, Long Island. My friend had induced his father to offer me a job as political columnist for the Hearst papers. The terms — large salary, big expense account, a roving commission, freedom to write as I saw fit and have it published — were glittering. "But Mr. Hearst," I said, "in a year at the most you would wish you had never employed me and I would, too." When we met again, in something less than a year, he said he had been reading my *New York Times* column attentively and I was right on both points of my prophecy.)

Though Bryan was making his third bid for the presidency, Democratic leaders who had opposed his first two candidacies were united behind him. But I think some — Henry Watterson, for example — had fallen in line in the belief that Bryan would strike out for the third time and they would be rid of him as a presidential candidate forever. Nevertheless, being Kentuckians, once they sniffed the smoke of battle they plunged deeply into the fray, and somewhat to their surprise, Bryan carried the state with a margin of nine thousand votes out of five hundred thousand cast.

I recall distinctly my impressions of Taft when he spoke in a town in the Bluegrass region — his enormous girth, his slightly hoarse voice and a countenance so beaming and a laugh so jolly that it seemed nothing could dissipate his good nature.

Several years later, after he was President, this impression dissolved in the heat of an anger to whose explosion I was a very surprised witness, under conditions, however, that oblige me to supply no details. But, though I also remember his campaign song at the meeting in the Bluegrass town, I can recall nothing of the issues he expounded. The words, to the tune of "Harrigan, That's Me," were approximately as follows:

B, I, double L, Y
T, A, F, T — that's his name.
We're proud of all the honesty that's in him,
Divil a bit a man can say agin him.
B, I, double L, Y
Tee-ee A, F, T.
He's a man that no shame ever could be connected
 with,
Billy Taft for me.

(At the Democratic National Convention of 1952 at Chicago, a parody, to the same tune, extolled the presidential aspiration of W. Averell Harriman.)

I was one of the *Herald* reporters who covered the great Democratic rally for Bryan at the First Regiment Armory in Louisville, and the congenital glamour which somehow invests the leaders of that party was apparent in full force. The color that Repub-

licans for some reason seem to lack was provided
by the dashing personalities and thrilling rhetoric
of Watterson, of Carmack of Tennessee (whom
Watterson introduced as "the Rupert of the Senate"),
and, finally, of the candidate himself. The certain
magic which nature lent to Bryan's voice, his handsome presence, the black forelock that fell across his
forehead at every climax of his prose — all these
were on display. But once again, except for the lordly
manner in which Watterson ignored the record of
his long and intense opposition to Bryan's presidential aspiration, I fail to remember the campaign
issues projected by the orators.

Next day I was drafted to drive Bryan across the
Ohio River to New Albany, Indiana, where he was to
address a devoted Hoosier constituency. When
Bryan estimated that our car had reached the point
of midstream under the bridge, he said: "Now we
are entering Indiana." "No, sir," I said, proud of my
pedantry, "under the Virginia grant of the Northwest
Territory the boundary of Kentucky is low-water
mark on the Indiana shore."

Many years later I discovered that President Lyn-
don B. Johnson had only minimal knowledge of
President Lincoln's suspension of the writ of habeas
corpus and the subsequent controversy. Recalling
the conversation with Bryan, I realized how pre-

posterous it was for me to expect that because a citizen aspired to the presidency, he would be familiar with those details of American history that happened to have lodged in my eccentric memory.

CHAPTER TWELVE

I WAS PERFORMING well enough as state editor
when the economy cut on the *Herald* sent me
looking for another job. At that point newly elected
Democratic city and county administrations were
ousted by Kentucky's highest tribunal, the Court of
Appeals, for proved election frauds, and A. Scott
Bullitt, a fellow Princetonian and warm personal
friend, was appointed interim sheriff of Jefferson
County. He named me as his personal deputy, and
for a couple of months I had a glorious time as an
officer of law enforcement against gambling and
such other pleasant local diversions as stuffing ballot
boxes. The salary was no less than that paid me by
the *Herald*, and moreover, though still required to
shave only about twice a week, I had the pleasant
sense of entering upon maturity by reason of the
lawful possession of a revolver which I wore thrust
conspicuously in my belt.

But being a deputy sheriff was not all fun, as
one grim incident of my service discloses. A young

countryman, in Louisville on a spree, had, under the influence of more whiskey than he could handle, murdered in a whorehouse three girls he accused of stealing his money. I was assigned by Sheriff Bullitt to visit the boy in jail, after he had been condemned to be hanged, to see if there was any consolation within the county's power that might ease the horror of his impending fate.

Yes, there was one, he said, after we had talked several times: he would go to his death with more peace of mind if I would attend his hanging. Since I had never before been confronted with the prospect of such an ordeal, I stalled for time, though subconsciously already aware I could not be so craven as to refuse him. For here was a normally peaceful lad — he was twenty-three years old — who had the misfortune of being one of those that alcoholic excess (second only to hard drugs) transforms into raging animals.

I still cringe at the memory of that morning when, at six o'clock, I met him at the foot of the gallows. We shook hands, he smiled and waved at me as he ascended to the platform and I had to force myself to remain there during the adjustment of the noose and the fitting of the mask, followed by the ghastly and simultaneous thump of the trapdoor when it opened and the crack of his neckbone as he fell.

His name need not be given here: it is carved on a

gravestone in a Kentucky village. But I hope it appears on a record beyond human sight. And if there is any substance in the Judeo-Christian ethic of divine mercy, there must be such a calendar.

But the ad interim status of Sheriff Bullitt and his deputies made it necessary for me to have another job in sight against our official terminal date only five months away. I enlisted some fellow reporters to look out for prospective openings in the newspaper business to which, with the passage of every day "in public office," I had found myself increasingly yearning to return.

It was not long before my scouts reported that there was an opening in the Louisville Bureau of the Associated Press and that J. H. Smythe, the correspondent (to whom they had grossly exaggerated my journalistic capabilities) wanted to talk to me about it. Not much more than half an hour after receiving this information I was in the presence of Mr. Smythe. After a personal inspection and a discussion of duties, both so cool that my feet sank to the same temperature, he unexpectedly offered me the job of night correspondent.

My duties were these:

I took over the desk at seven P.M., condensed and selected the dispatches which came over four night wires from the Chicago office to fit the capacity of the two wires with which the Louisville office served

the South and Mexico; and wrote, for dispatch on
the wires north and south, such news of city and
state origin as my superiors at Chicago and Atlanta
ordered from the brief summaries I sent them. The
tasks of condensation and selection called for an
editor-copyreader of experience and caliber far beyond my own — particularly since it was mandatory
that the southbound wires include reports of the
New York Stock Exchange, plus every foreign dispatch for the AP clients in Mexico. In about half a
year I acquired enough competence to muddle along
with this job and avoid getting fired.

But I had no editorial assistance, and my "staff"
consisted only of the telegraphers and a strong, over-
grown office boy whose justified rating of my professional skill was not very high. This culminated
in an act of insubordination I could not overlook
without losing my self-respect and my authority.

The act consisted of a sudden refusal to perform
the nightly chore of bringing sandwiches and beer
from a saloon nearby that the youth had not caviled
at before. Perhaps the sap of spring infused him
with a revolt against what had become to him
an act beneath his dignity. Or perhaps the cause was
rooted in the capricious nature which makes the Irish
so charming — his name was Frank McGuire. At
any rate, on my reiteration of the order, which he
asserted was "slave labor," he added: "Make me if

you can." So there was nothing for it but to accept the challenge.

We moved into the hallway, out of the visual range of the enchanted telegraph operators. At the outset it was plain that, though I was the less muscular vessel, Frank knew nothing at all about boxing, whereas I had been given a few pointers by Marvin Hart of Louisville, very briefly the heavyweight champion of the world.

The battle was short: I soon "drew claret," as the British say; we both agreed to lay down our arms, figuratively and practically; and Frank departed for and returned from his errand peaceably.

The incident lent me a certain prestige with the telegraphers, among whom there usually is a misanthrope whose cynicism is contagious. And I gained a degree of self-confidence in an executive role that afterward stood me in good stead. Therefore, here's to you, Frank McGuire — or your shade if, unlike me, you have, as in Dr. Holmes's poem, not "lived to be / The last leaf upon the tree / In the spring" — in other words, a superfluity.

I should mention that the saloon next door, Larry Gatto's, which supplied the sandwiches, was another of those in Louisville where good conversation and free lunch were to be found in generous measure. They were not inns such as the one celebrated by John Keats. But their gratified patrons would as quickly have answered in the affirmative the poet's question: "What Elysium have ye known / Happy field or mossy cavern / Choicer than the Mermaid Tavern?"

The responsibilities of the Associated Press Bureau in Louisville were greater and more numerous than those in cities of comparable size. In addition to the difficult professional task of consolidating the input of four wires from the Chicago office for transmission on two wires to the South and Mexico, while retaining all the important news, our crew of three was constantly under the captious eyes of our masters in the Chicago and Atlanta headquarters. Chicago delivered its vast product and scanned our Southern and Mexican newspaper clients for an evaluation of how well we had consolidated it. Atlanta happily handled any complaints from these clients, making sure Chicago knew of them. Between its two masters the Louisville Bureau was given a hard time.

But we got a fair share of praise. And the fact that we kept our jobs was sufficient evidence of reasonably good work. Under Smythe, the chief correspondent, were Charles T. Rogers on the day side and I on the night. Both my colleagues were first-rate at their trade, and I learned a lot about general reporting because, when major news broke in our provinces — Kentucky and Southern Indiana — the field work devolved on me.

Charlie Rogers, however, was the only one of the trio who had been touched by the Muses. He became a protégé of Richard Watson Gilder, who published a number of his poems in the *Century*. And, though I have known and worked with some of the most accomplished of those whose reporting now and then effortlessly attained the level of literature, I would place Rogers among the best.

He was a tall, lank Hoosier. His lantern face wore a sad expression, even though he was a pleasant companion in off hours. His contemporary hero was his father, a doctor in practice across the Ohio River in Jeffersonville, Indiana, who was repeatedly mentioned in dispatches by his Union commanders in the War Between the States; and by virtue of this association Charlie Rogers was an authority in detail on the battles in that conflict. After I left Louisville and the AP for Washington, he and I devotedly maintained our friendship, so that I knew the course he traveled to his tragic end as he was treading it.

After a long epistolary love affair with a girl in a burlesque stock company — epistolary because she was in Louisville only a week in the year — Rogers transferred his affections and married a pretty young lady from a rural Kentucky county who longed more for life in the metropolis than for Rogers as a husband. The depth and brilliance of his mind were beyond her comprehension, and they soon parted.

Being a romantic, Rogers was deeply damaged in spirit by this experience. He gave up his job, somehow eked out a dismal existence by selling a poem or an article here and there, and took heavily to the bottle. So it came about that he was living in a squalid room in a cheap lodging house when fate exacted from him the price which those with nobility of character must often pay in an unjust world.

A fellow lodger was a streetwalker, not very successful at her trade. She was given to melancholy, and, observing this and knowing the incidence of suicide, Rogers induced her always to talk away her troubles as part of a wholly platonic relationship. One night the lodging house caught fire, Rogers gained the street easily, looked for the girl and, not finding her, rushed back into the flames. He rescued her; she suffered no serious injury; but Rogers was fatally burned. After weeks in hospital, lying in a saline bath, he died in agony — the greater because his beautiful mind remained unimpaired until he ceased to breathe.

Smythe, our boss, was a professional of the first rank. But this side of him was virtually all that Rogers or I knew. He was taciturn of speech; whatever emotions he had he concealed, even in instances where another journalist in his position — we are an

outgiving breed — would have indicated anger, cha-
grin, disappointment, satisfaction, a gleam of personal affection or distaste. But he was as fair a man
in his judgment of the work of his subordinates as
any master I have served. And in consideration of
the number and exacting nature of his assignments,
he was as good as they come in his business.

In the histories of the American press, the first
two decades of this century are generally characterized as the concluding period of "personal journalism." By this term is meant that the editorial "we"
was unmistakably "I"; that the editor's individual
biases determined what was published in the news
columns with respect to events involving these
biases; and that the same was true of headlines and
the placement of the news. "Personal journalism"
was indeed a fair description of the character of
many of the leading newspapers. Watterson, as an
example, occasionally signed "H.W." to an editorial,
a practice which was far from uncommon.

But only when reporters and subeditors got spe-
cific policy instructions from the top were the news
columns slanted in any of these ways. The prevailing
instruction to reporters was to present the news factually, without editorial adjectives or tricks of colora-
tion. To Associated Press reporters and editors not
even a minute departure from this formula was permitted, and a deliberate infraction could mean the

loss of a job or a painful period of verifiable repent-
ance. This discipline was made more certain by the
fact that any infraction was certain to bring a protest
to the AP management from one or more of its newspaper clients.

CHAPTER THIRTEEN

I BECAME AWARE of the art, profession, trade or
con game known as politics when I was very
young, for politics seems to have been bred in the
bone of Kentuckians ever since the Commonwealth
was admitted into the Union, June 1, 1792. The
implant may not be deeper than in a number of
other states. But it was made highly tangible in
my childhood by constant reminders, ranging from
heated political discussions in my family circle and
the public places where citizens were wont to gather,
to frequent torchlight processions and the inevitable
shootouts at the polls.

Torchlight processions, with their flaunting banners, have gone out of style with the development
of new political technologies, culminating in the in-
vention of radio and television, and the turning away
from vituperative journalism. But the rival parades
— for supporters of opposing candidates shared the
demonstrations — were public entertainments which
provided a direct contact between office-seekers and

the voters that no performance on television or in a
large hall can supply. And almost gone, too, is the
"whistle-stop" campaign train where presidential
candidate and voters came intimately together every
few miles. (For this the jet airplane and the recent
outbreak of political assassinations are reponsible.)

I doubt that any of the modern rituals of politics
can produce the excitement over an election that was
evoked in a small town when the rising sound of
hoofbeats materialized in a file of torchbearing horse-
men, riding at full gallop, shouting the name of the
candidate of their choice.

By the time I was conscious of matters political,
the date in August for the election of Commonwealth
and county officials in Kentucky had been moved to
November, to conform with national practices. But
party nominations were still made in summer, and,
since the Democratic candidates then chosen were
virtually certain of election, these usually were occasions which rivaled the annual advent of the circus
as public entertainments.

That quality was largely the contribution of the
Negroes in the community. Those who owned their
land as well as those who worked for a landlord
brought produce to town, or to the rural polling
places, in horse-drawn carts and wagons drawn by
mules. On tables set up around the Court House
Square the Negroes offered for sale cantaloupes,

watermelons in their most delicious prime, gumbo, chicken, roast lamb and mutton, barbecued ribs, corn cakes, sweet cakes, homemade bread and cider — all of which found a ready and lucrative market. Eating was done to the rollicking strains of the fiddle and banjo, and in the pleasing sights of the hoedown, the pea-vine, the cakewalk and other gymnastic dances for which Negroes have a talent whites cannot match.

For boys, white and black, town and country types, the day imparted sheer bliss which even a rare spell of bad weather could not completely dispel. The pleasure was enlivened by a commendable number of fistfights between acknowledged champions of both races and of town and countryside. Only when some elders, made belligerent by whiskey, fell to physical combat to decide arguments and demonstrate political loyalties were these fistfights serious affairs. And when they reached this status, Town Marshal Winston Collins promptly afforded the combatants the hospitality of the town jail.

Rarely in our community was there an election-day shootout that called for his more drastic measures, though these were prevalent in other sections of the commonwealth. Then Collins did not hesitate to deal with the offenders by whatever means were required to enforce the law and maintain order.

The history of Kentucky is at the web and woof of the history of the United States. At one time or another, nearly all the issues that perplex and divide the American people, and now have brought the nation into the shadow of anarchy, were raised and more or less resolved in laboratory form in Kentucky. At least this was the situation when I was growing up in Glasgow and when I was a newspaper worker in Louisville.

Thus Kentucky was: The focal point of discovery westering from the Atlantic coast. The site of the original settlements which brought the white man's civilization to territory embroiled in the fierce internecine Indian wars. A fulcrum of the bloody struggle evoked by Secession. Initiator of the controversy over state versus Federal powers, and of resistance to corporate oppression by agricultural producers. Avant-garde of the wars which drove the French and British from the Colonies. Situs of the first state constitution which established suffrage as a right and not a privilege of land-owners. A center of the national political controversy over bimetallism. Cradle of the experiment of local and then national prohibition of alcoholic beverages. And pioneer in raising many other issues which have rent American public opinion, not excluding the practical proscription of Roman Catholics from high public office that is now a thing of the past.

The history of the Commonwealth is so rich, varied and significant that no attempt will be made to review it in depth in this place. Sufficient to my purpose will be to concentrate on the history, topography, sociology, politics and ecology of a small corner of Kentucky that includes the "Barrens," the burned-over land in the south central region — part of it in Barren County — where Virginia-derived small farmers became the social-economic median between the two extremes — the slaveholding plantation owners of the Bluegrass and the fierce Anglo-Celtic clans in the mountain areas in the eastern quadrant. But in passing, these general aspects of the history of the Commonwealth may be noted:

Although the popular majority in Kentucky was antislavery and anti-Secession in 1860, much of the territory south and west of the Green River was pro-Secession, though *ex post facto*. This area sent representatives to the Confederate Congress in Richmond; supplied many of Kentucky's ninety thousand troops in the Confederate Army, as contrasted with one hundred thousand in the Union; and would have officially carried Kentucky into the Confederacy if General Braxton Bragg, C.S.A., had not been dilatory in his advance toward Louisville. His delay allowed General Don Carlos Buell, the Federal commander, to get there first. And only by Buell's capture of this strategic point, after the indecisive battle of Perryville, was President Lincoln able to realize his most sentimental, also his vital military, goal — to keep his native state in the Union.

Just as the voyages of Columbus into the unknown western ocean were designed to find a sea route to the Orient, the early explorers of Kentucky proceeded on the theory that the Ohio River was the source of an inland water route to the Pacific. In consequence, Kentucky became the first settlement west of the Alleghenies. La Salle visited the Falls of the Ohio (later the site of Louisville) in 1669. Dr. Thomas Walker, for his Loyal Land Company, entered Kentucky through the Cumberland Gap in 1750. Christopher Gist and Alexander Scott Bullitt of Virginia surveyed the falls in the same year. And the lone search down the Wilderness Trail by John Finley in 1752 provided the lure that brought young Daniel Boone from North Carolina into Kentucky, via the Gap, in 1767.

An old American jest was that roosters lay eggs in Kansas, an illustration of the boasts of its pioneers. But the following are facts: The grass in Central Kentucky has a bluish tint when, in spring, the seed vessels are in bloom — hence the Bluegrass. The seven rivers which enter the Ohio in Kentucky flow northward. The sinkholes which abound in the Barrens cover underground streams which flow through the numerous caverns, such as Echo River in the stupendous Mammoth Cave, only seventeen miles from Glasgow, where the fish in these streams are blind. And an unusual number of towns and villages have names imported from the Eastern Hemisphere.

There is a rhyme:

> He went from Paris to Versailles,
> Gosh, but he was lucky.
> He rode to London, on the rails —
> And never left Kentucky.

In addition to which there are Glasgow, Moscow, Warsaw, Berlin, Cadiz, Frankfort, Tarascon, Lancaster, Dublin, Manchester, Winchester, Ravenna, Devon, Lebanon, Dundee, Brandenburg, and on, and on.

Also in the realm of fact: It was the new Commonwealth of Kentucky, firstborn of Virginia, that Jefferson chose for the proclamation of the Doctrine of Interposition. Using the Federalist Alien and Sedition Acts as his points of departure, Jefferson employed the Kentucky legislature to declare (the Kentucky Resolutions) that "the several States" which live under the Federal Constitution, "being sovereign and independent," have the final right to judge whether a Federal act infracts it, and, if so deciding, to nullify the act by nonenforcement within their jurisdictions.

First, Andrew Jackson forcibly repudiated this doctrine in his stand against Nullification; then it was deeply buried by the victory of the North in the War Between the States, to rise only briefly in Virginia's early resistance to the 1954 Supreme Court's ban on compulsory racial segregation of the public schools.

Kentucky from its assumption of statehood adhered to the Democratic-Republican party founded by Jefferson until the end of the presidential dynasty he established, and then supported Andrew Jackson and *his* Democratic party in the election of 1828. But with the second presidential challenge by Henry Clay — this time against the reelection of Jackson in 1832 — Kentucky turned to its famous native son and his Whig party. In this allegiance it remained until, the Whig party having dissolved on the rocks of the slavery issue, Kentucky returned to the Democratic fold, its allegiance punctuated by the split over bimetallism at the outset of the Eighteen Nineties (in 1895 its first Republican Governor was elected, and in 1896 most of its electoral votes were cast for the Republican presidential candidate, William McKinley). In national elections the state majority has since fluctuated rather regularly between the two major parties.

But while I was growing up, when the terms "Republican" and "radical" were interchangeable, there were parts of the Commonwealth where, if you called a man a Republican, it was the better part of valor to smile.

The late "Colonel" Mulligan made one exception in his paean to Kentucky: its politics, he wrote, was "the damnedest" anywhere.* In the years when I was a close observer of this folkway I disagreed with the Colonel only in thinking that the award should have gone to Indiana. But though the infighting among Hoosier politicians seemed to me even more lethal, the choice is a close one.

Two of my uncles made me aware of politics at an early age. Edward, the one who was Glasgow's first mayor, a Democratic partisan who believed his party could do nothing wrong and the "radicals" (Republicans) nothing right, assured me that the Republican gubernatorial nominee in 1899, William Taylor, and his family were hillbillies whose presence in the Governor's mansion was an indignity to the state; that the first time Mrs. Taylor wore shoes was when she put them on as the train which

---

* Songbirds are sweetest, in Kentucky,
Thoroughbreds the fleetest, in Kentucky;
The mountains tower proudest,
Thunder peals the loudest,
The landscape is the grandest,
And politics the damnedest,
    in Kentucky.
                    — "In Kentucky," by James Hilary Mulligan

bore her husband and her to his inauguration was crossing the Kentucky River into the capital city of Frankfort.

Taylor had been elected on the face of the returns; there was a contest; Taylor was deposed; and his Democratic rival, William Goebel, was sworn in as Governor while he lay dying from the bullet of an assassin. I had absorbed enough of this atmosphere of what was virtually a civil war to believe my uncle implicitly. And at the mature age of twelve I enthusiastically joined in chanting the derogatory slogans against Taylor and the "radicals."

In the course of the deadly bipartisan feud which followed the assassination of Goebel, my uncle Herman, who was city attorney, induced Negroes not to go to the polls because there were threats against those who did so. But before champions of equal rights who may read this book ring their loudest bell, hurl their angriest book, light their hottest candle, and proceed to excommunicate a community where this could have happened, let me add that in the Nineteen Sixties a Negro was chosen mayor of Glasgow; Negro voting has been unimpeded there for half a century; and a long-traditional two-thirds Democratic majority in Glasgow and Barren County has turned the other way in several elections for Governor and United States Senator, always when John Sherman Cooper was the Republican candidate.

Moreover, the progress has come without the stigma of the deadly violence that was averted on that election day in the Eighteen Nineties by my uncle's "pragmatic sanction."

When in 1907, on the *Louisville Herald*, I got my first assignments as a backup political reporter the dominant Democratic party of Kentucky was sharply divided into two factions. The leader of the wing which would now be termed "liberal" was John Crepps Wickliffe Beckham, who was Goebel's running mate and succeeded to the governorship when Goebel died after taking the oath of office. The leader of the wing which now would be termed "conservative" was General William Birch Haldeman, the editor in chief of the *Louisville Times* and part owner of the *Times* and the *Courier-Journal*.

John Crepps Wickliffe Beckham, invariably spoken of as "Cripps," was tall, courtly and floridly handsome, a fitting representative of the aristocratic line from which he descended: at one time two of its members were concurrently Governor of Kentucky and of Louisiana. Self-identified as a reformer of political mores which could surely stand reforming, he nevertheless was their unprotesting beneficiary.

He was well educated, as his speech reflected; and his accent was the kind of moderate Southern, with the soft "r" which is pleasing to the ear. He dressed with taste and care, and bore himself with quiet dignity. But he had a drinking problem, a point of vulnerability that, sometimes noticeable in public occasions, was seized on by adversaries who drank as much or more but had the good fortune to possess hollow legs, as the saying goes. My final dealings with Beckham were in his tenure as a United States Senator, and, despite my identification with newspapers which constantly attacked him, I was the recipient of the most extreme courtesy on his part.

General Haldeman (the rank deriving from a period of command of the Kentucky National Guard) had served in the Confederate forces, leaving his studies at the Kentucky Military Institute to join the Confederate Navy as a midshipman. In manner, physical appearance, gallantry and turn of speech he was the very prototype of the legendary Kentuckian. The General was very tall; his hair was plentiful, even after it turned white; he wore a mustache and the traditional goatee; his eyes were bluer than blue; and his complexion radiated energy and good health. A lover of the thoroughbred horse, he was a daily spectator at the Louisville tracks, and his money was riding on every race.

There were reports that just after the Confederate war, the General had gone to Palestine, Texas, and competed successfully with the cactus frontier gamblers who were widely known for high-stake poker games and quickness of the draw — a reputation which Haldeman said nothing to contradict. But, these wild oats sown, he obeyed his father's demand to come home and take his due part in the operation of the *Courier-Journal* and the *Times*. When I first met him he was editor in chief of the *Times* and a director of the Courier-Journal Company that owned both newspapers.

General Haldeman's principal professional rival was Richard W. Knott, editor of the *Evening Post*, and warmly allied to the Beckham faction. While the *Post*, being an afternoon newspaper, directed the bitter flame of its rhetoric against the *Times*, its afternoon competitor and the unit of the Courier-Journal Company for which General Haldeman was directly responsible as editor in chief, Knott also pursued a personal vendetta against Haldeman. Unfortunately for Knott, his physical differences from the tall, handsome, urbane Haldeman could not have been more marked, for in addition to an unprepossessing visage, the *Post* editor was lame in one leg.

In the *Times* office they delighted in an incident which emphasized these circumstances. As Timesmen told the story, Haldeman one day was walking down a corridor when he became aware of a fluttering disturbance at his coattails. Turning, and beholding Knott flailing his fists in the air, Haldeman gently inquired what his fellow editor was doing.

"I'm fighting you, sir," said Knott. "Nonsense," said Haldeman, and proceeded calmly on his way.

His father, Walter N. Haldeman, owned a newspaper called the *Courier*, merged it with the *Journal*, of which the celebrated George D. Prentice was owner-editor, and in 1869 chose the rising celebrity Henry Watterson as editor of the *Courier-Journal*. Both the elder Haldeman and Watterson were supporters of the Confederacy, and during the War Between the States each published a newspaper behind the Confederate lines — Watterson's was called the *Chattanooga Rebel*. From this background the General emerged as the political leader of the conservative Democratic faction in Louisville and the state. Of his two younger brothers, Bruce Haldeman became the president and publisher of the Courier-Journal Company; John Haldeman, who died in comparative youth, was an officer of the corporation and so was the only Haldeman sister, Belle.

The division between the Haldeman and Beckham factions was permanent and bitter, but conflicting political ideology was not involved. For example, Goebel, whom both the Beckham group and the *Courier-Journal* and *Times* strongly supported, merited the classification of "the First New Dealer," given him by Urey Woodson, an Owensboro editor who later was secretary of the Democratic National Committee. Instead, the factional struggle was for

offices and the power that went with them. And
though the Jockey Club and the whiskey distillers
were the targets of the Beckhamites, on the ground
that their power at Frankfort was the evil product of
campaign contributions, they equally would have
been the targets of the rival faction if the contributions had gone into the other till.

The operator of the Beckham machinery was
Percy Haly, one of the shrewdest and most ruthless
politicians I ever knew but endowed with a personality which drew me to him personally.

Haly was also called "General," this because he
had served as Adjutant General. This illustrates the
Southern, and more particularly the Kentucky, custom of permanently entitling citizens who have held
office, or are leaders of the professions. Thus, at
functions both public and private, one heard such
introductions as "Miz Judge Jones, I want you to
meet Miz Colonel Smith" (or "Miz Doctor Brown,"
or "Miz Lawyer Green," etc.). But any prominent
lawyer is called "Judge." And as long as any Confederate soldier, whatever his rank, was alive, he was
addressed as "Colonel," "Major" or "Captain," according to his choice. (According to Representative
John Allen of Mississippi, he was "the only private
in the Confederate army.")

Whatever the reasons Haly's mother had for
naming him "Percy," no one less resembled the effete

London fop who invariably was entitled Percy in the caricatures and other humorous sketches of that period. Haly was rather short, unusually broad-shouldered, and walked with a slight stoop. He had a habit of holding his head to one side and looking out from half-lidded eyes, and this contributed to his reputation of being very sly. When he spoke the sound was like a light fall of gravel. But the effect of the combination was curiously attractive, accounting to some degree for the general impression of Haly as a man of mark. And this he repeatedly demonstrated in brilliant management of the political faction of which he was the field commander.

General Haldeman's operating deputy was former Mayor Charles E. Grainger of Louisville, and there was nothing he and Haly did not know about the vote-getting lures of politics. In one election the Haly organization voted the names of citizens who were not among the living: they were taken off the gravestones in the Frankfort cemetery. To match this, in the 1905 mayoralty election in Louisville, the candidate supported by the other faction not only received a unanimous vote in the Twelfth Ward, but the voters there miraculously cast their ballots in alphabetical order, beginning with Aa and ending with Zy.

In the gathering issue over national prohibition the Beckham machine was officially, though far from individually, "dry." Its rival group was both officially and individually "wet." The preachers and women of the state had already, through local option, effected prohibition in most of the counties. Hence the secret ballot was the only means available to the wife-and-clergy-ridden husbands and formal church-goers, who "voted dry and drank wet," to prevent a statewide ban on the distilling, possession and use of alcoholic beverages.

This emotional factor increased the normally high temperature of Kentucky politics, and shoot-outs at the rural polls were matters of course in every election. (As I write, this folkway has diminished almost to the vanishing point. But at least one vestigial shoot-out occurred at the poll for the election of a Governor in 1971.)

I got my foot in the door that opened on political reporting by making a good impression on the most famous occupant of the field in the state, John Dowds Wakefield, and also because of the circumstance that he maintained his headquarters in the *Herald* office. In this period his political articles, next to Henry Watterson's in the *Courier-Journal*, were the most widely read in Kentucky. They were published under his by-line on Sundays in the *Cincinnati Enquirer*, and my good fortune was that Wakefield's eye had lighted on me several times when he wanted some detail pertinent to his writing.

Our relation became a close friendship, and this

friendship in time brought me a triple bonus. The first was that Wakefield suggested to the City Editor that I was a good prospect for political reporting. The second was that he broadened my scope from local to national by borrowing me to serve as his legman at the Republican and Democratic national conventions of 1908, at Chicago and Denver respectively. The third was that, asked by Wakefield to take his telephone calls when he was out of the office, I became well acquainted with a cousin of his who was the most celebrated of the Kentucky beauties of the day — Mrs. Clarence Lebus.

A combination of all these fortuitous circumstances got me my first major assignment in the field of politics: reporting the gubernatorial election of 1907 in which Kentucky elected the second Republican Governor in its history, Augustus E. Willson.

Willson in every way was unlike his political contemporaries. He was a Harvard graduate (later an overseer of the university); a learned lawyer, but colorless at the bar; a reformer in a state which was disposed to look skeptically at this species. When intent on some problem, Willson had the habit of humming — hence the nickname "Hummy" with which the Democrats sought to disparage him. He was just barely a native Kentuckian in a Commonwealth to which this status was almost indispensable to election in his time, having been born on an Ohio

River flatboat docked at Maysville, of parents migrating from the East.

But his suppression of the Night Riders by the armed forces, reluctant though he was to resort to that, showed that Willson had a Presbyterian vein of iron. By the means he used to restore order to the tobacco fields, and especially because while Governor, in a speech at Harvard, he critically reviewed conditions in Kentucky, he made certain the loss of the state to the Democrats in the election of 1911.

Willson was a short, thick man, with a long equine countenance, yet possessed of a personal charm in private intercourse that he was unable to transmit in his official activities. But of the Kentucky Governors in modern times he was probably the best educated. This, however, led him into highly literary tropes and quotations that floated over the heads of many of his auditors. Nevertheless, he was instrumental in "moving Kentucky into the twentieth century" with respect to social problems. And though his substitution of plain speaking for political platitudes was brief — his Democratic successor as Governor, James B. McCreary, restored them in full force — it refreshed the electorate while it lasted.

I accompanied Governor Willson on his travels in the search of peace in the tobacco-growing areas where the price of tobacco had fallen so low that growers resorted to the violence known as "Night

Riding." The object of this was, by burning storage barns and despoiling crops, to force growers who sold their crops independently to join a "selling pool" formed by the others.

The result was a form of anarchy, attended by bloodletting. Governor Willson's efforts to restore order culminated in his call-out of the National Guard in 1908. But not until, by the legislative creation, in the early Nineteen Twenties, of a tobacco growers' cooperative, designed by Bernard M. Baruch at the request of the *Courier-Journal*, did a complete end come to the bloody war in the tobacco-growing areas in which, for a year or more, outrages were perpetrated every night against the recalcitrants.

An experience I had in reporting a speech by Governor Willson in Cadiz, in western Kentucky, illustrates the depth of the lawlessness evoked in this controversy. As I waited on the street before the speech was to begin, I saw a procession of men on horseback and in carriages who carried signs supporting the Night Riders. And heading this procession of leading citizens was the Democratic candidate for Congress in the district, later United States Senator, Ollie M. James.

James was a mountain of a man — six and a half feet tall and nearly three hundred pounds in weight. I recall that when — years later, in Washington — my wife saw him one evening attired in a yellow overcoat which surely had used up the hair of a score of Saharan camels, she remarked that he brought to mind the back of a taxicab going away. But James's physical dimensions, the fact that his voice was in proportion, and his uncanny ability as a political phrasemaker, made him the most effective stump-speaker of his time. And in the Senate, to which he progressed from representing the First Kentucky District in the Federal House of Representatives, he filled the galleries and did not disappoint them — particularly in the use of a gift of riposte that made it a risk for any Senator to challenge him.

But for all James's mastery of sophisticated politics not too far above the demagogic level, he had a high score for credulity. Flattery did not need to be subtle for him to swallow whole. On one occasion, assured that only he could save a state Democratic convention from control by the Haldeman faction, he nominated himself for chairman. "I give you," he told the delegates, "Ollie M. James, a Democrat who has never scratched the party ticket." (The convention replied, in effect, "No, thanks.")

He was deeply suspicious by nature, but not a very good judge of those toward whom his suspicion should be directed. Hence he was frequently imposed on and as frequently rebuffed a sincere well-wisher in the belief that the good man "had an angle," as they say in Newspeak.

In a previous book I have described how his passion for betting on horse races continuously prevailed over his expressed conviction that racing was "crooked" and that it was his duty to ban it by legislation. And, though it is a common phenomenon that one day's loser at the tracks is certain he will be next day's winner, none was stronger in this faith, and its practice, than James.

CHAPTER FOURTEEN

THE REMINISCENCES of the aged tend to stress the simplicity of American society in their youth as contrasted with present super-urban sophistication. But this transformation is no more remarkable than the fact that the cavemen had no electricity. All life is change, though its movement swings cyclically from the possession of too much to the possession of too little. And the regular reversion to the latter stage is normally the consequence of overindulgence in the former.

However, there may be some usefulness as well as interest in recording for later generations detail of life in the simpler American society that passed with the entrance of the United States into the First World War. What follows is based on this assumption.

Even before the day when Major Throckmorton, the imperious proprietor of the Galt House, ordered the equally imperious Charles Dickens to give up his lodging at the hotel, because that famous hostelry would not tolerate bad manners on the part of any

guest, however celebrated, Louisville was a sophisticated community. It may not have been the Boston
of the South, but it had a stronger claim to this than
upstart Atlanta, somnolent Charleston and pleasure-
centered New Orleans.

The Filson Club, founded by Colonel Reuben T.
Durrett, housed then and now the most authoritative
and comprehensive archive there is of the history of
the great migration to the West. The evenings of
the Salmagundi, devoted to literary discussion —
ancient and modern — and appreciative sipping of
fine French wines, were indeed "feats of reason and
flows of soul" by virtue of the brilliance and wide-
ranging culture of its carefully chosen members. And
if the term "gentleman" is held to its proper definition to mean a civilized, educated, well-mannered
man, then no club in the United States numbered
more such persons proportionate to its size than the
Pendennis. Moreover, wit and humor were in ample
supply in all these assemblages.

Yet though the élite of the town lived in fine
houses, set the best of tables, sent their offspring
to the leading preparatory schools and colleges of the
South and East, "brought out" their debutantes, regularly traveled abroad and repaired in season to the
seacoast, the mountains and the subtropics, the fa-
cilities they lived with and by were simple. House
servants were home-grown. The trolley car was the

standard means of transportation to places of business. It was considered pretentious for a hostess to require that guests to dinners and balls be announced by butlers. The parlor divertissments were simple, too. ("The Game," with its rival teams and sign-language, had not been invented.) The hostess who suggested an evening of such guessing games as "rivers beginning with an 'X,'" musical chairs or amateur theatricals was not deemed to be what now is termed "square" or addicted to "camp." There also were readings by the best-known local poet, Madison Cawein, and Alice Hegan Rice, the author of *Mrs. Wiggs of the Cabbage Patch.*

Guests frequently entertained one another with renditions of piano and violin music. And as frequently the evening was spent in the art of good conversation which, like the epistolary, has almost vanished from the American social scene. Nearly everybody had, or was, a cordon bleu cook, Southern style. And on the rare occasions when guests were not dined at home, no banquet fare was superior to that served by the Pendennis Club or one of the several restaurants which made the city a gourmet's delight.

The courting of the young usually included letters replete with quotations from the poets or, now and then, home-grown effusions. A girl who could show her friends an attempt at an original sonnet by a love-sick swain (this was not unusual) was sincerely envied. I know, since I "committed" more than a few metrical tributes to the girl of the moment. Sometimes the purpose of the verses was to try to gain from her the special interest that "poets" are supposed to arouse in the female breast. I suddenly recall — how and why I cannot possibly imagine — a turgid opus I committed at that period. Drunk on Kipling, the following (so help me!) lurched off my typewriter:

Down through the passes to Kandahar
Went the hill man, Khel, rejoicing.
Guided was he by the morning star
And his own glad spirit's voicing.

Azizun sat in her tower.
She watched the east where storm-clouds lower:
O'er all the hills the sunlight sped,
As her lone heart swung in hope, in dread —
Love's flower is white,
Love's flower is red.

In the pass of Jahil
Waited Murad Din.
In his heart black sin
Leapt and crept and cowered.
The black rock pass of Jahil
Roared with echoing shout —
Khel's merry voice rang out,
Making sin empower'd.

A thrust, a cry, a dripping knife
And in the darkness sank a life.
The hills sought Murad Din in flight:
Love's flower is red,
Love's flower is white.

In her tower Azizun
Waited yearning, tender,
Waited 'til the rising sun
Lifted lances slender.

Suns have risen, suns have set,
They who played this scene are dust,
But the shed blood wanders yet
Seeking vengeance as it must —
Though the crime is aeons dead:
Love's flower is white,
Love's flower is red.

(I proudly regard the line "Making sin empower'd" as a candidate for the worst line in the history of versification.)

There were many people of wealth and good taste in Louisville to give at-home dinner parties, augmented by dancing or musical recitals, large enough to require the regular service of a caterer. In "Mr. Solger," as he was known, the city had one worthy of having made up the menus of Lucullus. Mr. Solger's principal business was that of a confectioner: his store at Fourth and Broadway was always thronged with persons of all ages with a discriminating sweet

tooth. But Mr. Solger was also a deadpan social sat-
irist, and he affected to be a lineal descendant of
Sheridan's Mrs. Malaprop. To witness: Mrs. George
M. Davie, one of his constant patrons, was the wife
of the leader of the Louisville bar, as elegant of manner, ancient of breeding and cultivated as her husband. For several weeks she had been planning a very
large and important party, and, after each of numerous consultations with Mr. Solger in which menus
were firmly agreed on, Mrs. Davie as constantly
changed the entrée. Mr. Solger bore the first few
changes with patient fortitude, but the last was too
much for him. Although he knew well the meaning
and spelling of the word "enigma," he burst out:
"You society ladies are sure an enema to me!"

William Sydney Porter (O. Henry) once ended a
story with a speculation whether anything of note
ever happened in Nashville, Tennessee. And he wrote
a tale out of his imagination that recorded a very exciting Nashville happening indeed. But no fictional
talent was required to invest the Louisville of my
young reportorial days with an atmosphere which
was at once exciting and *gemütlich*, odd though this
combination may appear.

The unusual number of the celebrities in a town
of only two hundred and fifty thousand afforded
those made of commoner clay a sense of the nation's

history as they went about their daily affairs. For example, walking in Walnut Street, near Fourth, one was likely to see, sitting in the sun on the porch of the old Pendennis Club, Major Dan Wood, a huge old man with a demeanor so gentle, almost timid, that a stranger to the city would have been amazed to learn of him what the natives knew well — that his deeds as a cavalry officer under General Crook in the Indian wars were legendary in the Army.

And it was widely known, too, that the Major, when sufficiently refreshed by Boone's Knoll (he always had it served with "two glahsses" of water, neither of which he touched, for this would have been sacrilege to one of the noblest of the bourbons) always confused two themes in his anecdotes of conquest. In the midst of a tale of his famous solo ride to Fort Douglas in Arizona to summon troops for the relief of the besieged garrison at Fort Huachuca, during which he slew, successively, one, two, three and then a "band," of armed savages, and being disposed to doze in the midst of the telling, the Major, awakened with a demand for the climax, would reply: "Of course, she gave in about two o'clock in the morning."

The celebrities were to be encountered not only on the streets but in the streetcars, some of them still horse-drawn when I worked on the *Herald*, since nearly everyone — however distinguished — used

this means of transportation. It was an ordinary experience to ride downtown on a Fourth Street trolley
with the élite of the town in full evening dress. And
men unknown to one another would pass the time
of day with lifted hats, or women in bonnets imported from Paris nod to bareheaded shopgirls.
Louisville was, but is no more, a "Southern" town.

I recall that the streets were safe to the point
where a long walk home in the small hours was
made without a thought of danger: there was no
need. I did this regularly, and I particularly remember one occasion. Miss Viola Dana and her musical
comedy company were playing at Macauley's Theatre, and the press agent had induced two of the cast
to be married on the stage after a performance, with
a champagne supper to follow. Perhaps it was the
several libations we consumed *à deux* that plunged
the bride into a flood of tears and impelled me to feel
it my duty to lead her into a corner to be consoled; at
any rate, she did and I did. So that I started to walk
uncertainly to my lodging house a mile or so away,
at three A.M., an inviting target for any footpad. But
the only hazard involved, and it did not materialize,
was that I might mistake a sidewalk for the couch I
was heading for — a possibility my friend, Captain
Bright of the police, suggested to me when we met in
front of the Seelbach.

No community having been more deeply divided

than Kentucky in what was called simply "the War" (1861–1865) in my young days, Louisville had its quota of distinguished soldiers on both sides. It was these men who, more than anyone else, "bound the wounds" of at least this part of the nation; and who became fixtures in the city's social and political establishment.

Of these soldiers, none was more distinguished, or exemplified more the style that gave Louisville its own cachet, than John Breckinridge Castleman, major in the Confederate cavalry of General John Hunt Morgan, brigadier general in the Kentucky National Guard.

In family background, grace of manner and dazzling good looks he was the most glamorous citizen of Louisville. His height was well over six feet, his walk was military to the day of his death, his voice was as soft as his Bluegrass accent, and, like so many of his companions in arms, General Castleman wore the mustache and goatee that, as they silvered, accentuated the sparkle of bright blue eyes.

"I was born," he wrote in his memoirs, "in the season of the rose and the elder blossom, in June, at 'Castleton,' my father's house, in Fayette County, Kentucky" (of which Lexington is the proud seat). After Lee's surrender at Appomattox, Castleman, still a uniformed belligerent, fled to Canada, with a price on his head under charge as an armed rebel.

This, of course, was true of every man in Morgan's command as time after time it raided the towns of Ohio and Indiana in its role as the terror of the Union in those areas.

Not long after the end of the war, Castleman, under sentence as a "war criminal," was paroled by President Andrew Johnson and settled in Louisville. There he became one of the earliest of the urban developers in American history, and the creator of the city parks. And during his lifetime, which was long, the city paid him a unique tribute for his constructive citizenship. It placed a bronze equestrian statue of the General at the entrance to Cherokee Park. And on his morning walks he had the unique distinction of looking at his own memorial as he passed.

He did not live extravagantly — modestly in contrast with the lavishness which surrounded the family at "Castleton" — but his purse was open for every friend in need and many who were freeloaders. Consequently, he was often short of cash, and his general theory that the Lord will provide often required his creditors to wait beyond their patience. But except for this there was none in the community to fault him. As one example of his contributions to his time I particularly remember an incident early in the participation of the United States in the First World War, when I had become editorial manager of the *Courier-Journal* and the *Louisville Times*.

Camp Zachary Taylor, a unit in the structure of American war-preparedness, had been located on the outskirts of Louisville, and was a training center for aspirants to officer rank in the Field Artillery. These candidates were native to a number of states in the South and Midwest, and were directed by officers, headed by Major General Harry Hale, U.S.A., of the same diverse geographical derivation.

One day the word came to General Hale that the Army, in its infinite wisdom, was sending Colonel Benjamin Davis, an Inspector General, to perform his function at Camp Zachary Taylor. When the information spread to the officer group, a large number — including a few from the Midwest — respectfully advised General Hale that, if they encountered Colonel Davis, a Negro, they would not salute him. Hale telephoned me for any help I could suggest, explaining he was confronted with the serious prospect of having to put most of his officers on charges.

After some pondering, I telephoned to General Castleman, explained the situation, and asked if he could think of anything to say which would help Hale out of his predicament. Instantly he replied: "You may publish this: when General Castleman was advised of the threat of officers of the Army not to salute Colonel Davis if they encountered him, General Castleman said: 'I shall, of course, salute Colonel Davis if, as I trust, I shall encounter him.

A salute is to the uniform, not the man who wears it.' " I boxed this statement on page one of the *Courier-Journal* and the Camp Zachary Taylor "rebellion" ended before it began. For if "Breck" Castleman, Confederate hero, of the Kentucky blood royal, would unhesitatingly salute a Negro officer, who were they that dared to refuse?

More of a Confederate stereotype in some respects than Castleman was General Bennett H. Young. His title was largely honorific (I think he had been an adjutant general of the National Guard), for it was as a Confederate lieutenant that he acquired fame. Having escaped to Canada from Camp Douglas, after capture by Union troops in Ohio, he was commissioned by the Confederate government to manage the return to the South of Confederate military personnel who, like himself, had escaped from Federal prisons to Canada. In pursuit of this assignment, Young and a small Confederate band raided St. Albans, Vermont, and made off with the cash in the town banks, a minimum of fifty thousand dollars, with which he purchased supplies and shipping to transport his charges to their commands, via the West Indies. (After the war the United States government restored the fifty thousand dollars to the banks of St. Albans.)

A director of the Courier-Journal Company, Young represented the minority interests of John, a deceased Haldeman brother, and the one Haldeman daughter, Belle. In physical appearance Young was a walking portrait of the Confederate cavalryman — long-legged, slender, tall, mustachioed and goateed. In civil life he was also a police-court defense lawyer whose fiery rhetoric, though delivered in a soft accent, burned his targets to a crisp. Next to another lawyer, Sol Cain, of whom it was said that "he freed more Negroes than Lincoln,"* Young was a renowned champion of Negroes caught in the toils of the criminal law.

In the courtly manner of Judge William Overton Harris, dean of the University of Louisville Law School, there was nothing to suggest trial by battle. Yet Judge Harris had been one of the cadets of the Virginia Military Institute at Lexington (its prewar commandant was General Thomas J. [Stonewall] Jackson) who fought gallantly against the Federal troops on May 15, 1864, at Newmarket, in the Shenandoah Valley. The cadets were called on by General John Cabell Breckinridge, the Confederate commander, and with his forces they checked the advance up the Valley Pike of the Union troops under General Franz Sigel.

The effect of a host of such citizens was to inspire

* I am indebted to my old *Herald* colleague, Malcolm Bayley, for recalling to me this courtroom jest.

among the inhabitants of the town the kind of pride
that Paul expressed in Jerusalem (Acts 21: 39).
Bound in chains, and asked if he was not the Egyp-
tian who had caused an "uproar" in the community,
he replied that his birthplace was Tarsus, in Cilicia,
"no mean city." And the Louisville man-in-the-street
was known to tell strangers that an unusual number
of stars of lesser magnitude also lived in the town or
spent a part of the year there.

On Main Street one might see, emerging from the
offices of a wholesale leather company, a tall, erect,
ruddy, white-maned individual whose erect military
bearing was in such sharp contrast to the humdrum
nature of his business that it was not surprising to
learn he had commanded a Union battery on Little
Round Top at Gettysburg — Andrew Cowan his
name. In Jefferson Street, among those leaving a
building largely occupied by lawyers, an acquaintance could pass the time of day with Major Adolphus
E. Richards, an old man so gentle in speech and
manner that it was difficult to envisage him as one
of the most daring lieutenants of Colonel John Sin-
gleton Mosby, C.S.A., who had hanged seven of
General Custer's cavalrymen in retaliation for the
hanging of seven Mosby men by General Philip
Sheridan. And in the lobby of the Galt House, east-
ward of Main Street, there was often to be found an
unusually tall, white-bearded lodger whose slight

stoop was his only concession to great age — Simon Bolivar Buckner, up from his home in the rural county of Hart. Yet in his youth he had been a principal in a vital episode of the War Between the States: he had surrendered Fort Donelson to General Grant only after his senior officers had deserted him and his supplies ran out. And he had been the nominee for Vice President of the United States on the Democratic Gold Party Ticket in 1896. (His hobby was fashioning corncob pipes — he sent them regularly to me, the grandson of an old friend and neighbor.) And in a classroom of Centre College, in Danville, were gathered the students of Professor James C. Willson, who, after the War, rode there from Virginia with almost his sole possessions a degree from the University at Charlottesville and a letter to this effect: "I have served four years in the Confederate Army with James Willson, and in every way — in honor, courage, character, loyalty and scholarship — I commend him to the favor of whomsoever he may encounter. [signed] Robert E. Lee."

Nor did Louisville's reputation rest on this collection of distinguished old soldiers. Intellectually and culturally, the town made a national contribution.

Perhaps the shabbiest law office in Louisville was one near the Court House, yet the leaders of the bar beat a path to its door. For there was to be found Louis Dembitz, a gnome of an old man, one of the most learned members of the American bar in his time, whose nephew, Associate Justice Louis Dembitz Brandeis of the Supreme Court of the United States, was also a native of Louisville. Dembitz was deeply respected, unafraid of anything or anybody, unconventional in act and manner, a lawyer's lawyer. Once, consulted on a difficult case by the prominent attorney George M. Davie, Dembitz listened to Davie's outline of how he would handle the matter and, peering at Davie through his thick spectacles, quietly remarked: "I think you are a damned fool." "Watch your language or I'll throw you out of the window," said Davie. "You'll still be a damned fool," replied Dembitz.

Other Louisville natives were Simon Flexner, the great pathologist who devised the serum for cerebrospinal fever which reduced its mortality rate by two-thirds, and his brother Abraham, who became one of the most famous educational authorities in the nation. With Dembitz and Brandeis they were members of a group of Louisville Jews, descendants of Spanish-Portugese immigrants to the Thirteen Colonies, who lent high distinction to the community.

Alexander Prather Humphrey was foremost among the city's lawyers, since he led the Kentucky bar for the longest period covered by any attorney in the state. A small man, highly cultured, he was one of the few Americans who have rejected a Cabinet appointment. When President Taft offered him the portfolio of Secretary of War, Humphrey overcame the temptation to accept by not telling his wife of the offer, fearing she would insist that he take it.

Humphrey's unique professional distinction was reflected in a Louisville jest about the only means by which a newcomer could even hope to attain social status: "Join Christ Church, open an account in the Bank of Kentucky, buy a lot in Cave Hill cemetery and hire Aleck Humphrey as your lawyer." As general counsel of the Southern Pacific Railway, Humphrey, for tax reasons, set up the headquarters of the giant corporation in a small cottage near Louisville, to be used for a few hours once a year for the railway system's annual meetings.

He was counsel for Watterson in the celebrated contest involving the control of the *Courier-Journal* and the *Louisville Times*. Watterson, General W. B. Haldeman and Belle Haldeman, children of the founder, had deposed Bruce Haldeman, a brother, from the presidency of the company and the latter had cited a contract which, he contended, made the action invalid. Successfully pleading for the rejection of this contention, Humphrey dramatized the fact that Watterson's ownership share amounted to only eight per cent of the total by exclaiming: "A miserable pittance for a contribution that has been indelibly engraved on the tablets of great journalism."

Gastronomically, too, Louisville was celebrated afar. The fame of the ancient Pendennis Club for excellent food, drink, conviviality and quality of service was on a national scale in the many years the club inhabited a fine old converted private house in Walnut Street across from Macauley's Theatre. (The Pendennis has long since removed to a modern three-story building.) Supervising the dining rooms was a headwaiter whose port and dignity were no less than those of any similar functionary in the clubs along St. James's Street. His name was Henry Bain, and members or guests guilty of any lapse of manners — such as loud talk or obstreperousness — usually were quelled by his disapproving glance.

When Henry Bain let it be known to particular friends among the members that he had a talented nephew he hoped to launch on a career, it was taken as a privilege to assist him. By this means the nephew was sent to the Juilliard School of Music in New York, and eventually, as Roland Hayes, became an outstanding American singer of spirituals and songs of the great German, Italian and French composers — in their original languages.

A good deal of the aura of a town, of course, depends upon the pleasures and entertainments it affords and the wit it sustains. Louisville offered a variety that extended from the elegant to the broad.

The staff of the Pendennis Club included an official wag, a sort of Chicot (the impudent jester of Henry III of France), who the members believed could hold his own with any member of the *cap-and-bells* fraternity anywhere. His name was Lonny Elliott. He had a knack of taking liberties with the members who patronized his domain, the billiard room, in so elusive a way that the victim had to laugh at himself or be forever set down as a stuffed shirt. An example of Elliott's bloodless skinning occurred during the First World War.

A member of the club, George Lindenberger, was very sensitive about the impression of many in the town that, because of his name, dark complexion and Semitic nose, he was of the Hebrew race, though actually he was a scion of the colonial "Pennsylvania Dutch" who migrated to Virginia and made garden-spots of the areas in which they settled. Lindenberger arrived in the crowded billiard room, together with the delivery of the *Louisville Times* which that day bore the headline: "ALLENBY ENTERS JERUSALEM." Thrusting a copy of the paper at him, Elliott softly said: "Mr. George, your home town done fell."

Haute cuisine is not usually associated with the cloister. And Gethsemane is a Trappist monastery near Louisville, where the vows of total silence and absolute poverty are strictly observed by the hair-shirted monks, and infractions are heavily punished by their shepherd. But from these obligations, in my time, the Abbot of Gethsemane, Father Obrecht, held himself immune. With his favorite guest, Commonwealth Attorney Joseph Huffaker, he shared an appreciation of, and expertise toward, food and drink, and these were expressed in gargantuan banquets at the monastery. While silent monks served the gourmet dinners, the Abbot and his guests made the rafters ring, as the saying goes, with uninhibited songs and conversation. I don't know with what nickname Father Obrecht addressed the Commonwealth Attorney, but Huffaker's for the Abbot was "the Turtle," explaining that the good prelate "traveled on his belly."

In every city the keepers of the best taverns are men of mark, and very much so in Louisville were the brothers Louis and Otto Seelbach. They were proprietors of the hotel that, after "modernization," again bears their name; its main dining rooms and rathskeller were nationally famous for the excellence of menus and service; and the Seelbachs were equally so for the warmth and good taste of their hospitality, conveyed in the soft accent with which the many Louisville citizens of Swabian ancestry spoke English.

"Louie," as he was informally known, was a giant in stature — perhaps six feet and a half — in contrast to his average-size brother. Of Louie's two sons, the elder, Louie, Jr., had his father's dimensions, and Willie, the younger, those of his uncle Otto. Willie was fleet of foot and Louie was a physical powerhouse: hence, as a tackle and a halfback on the football team of Centre College in Danville, Kentucky, which was to achieve fame as the Praying Colonels that beat Harvard, they formed a destructive combination when teamed in play. One day Louie, Sr., who attended all of Centre College's games, decided that to use the filial combination was the only means to avert impending defeat. Rising in the stands to his towering height, and employing the bullhorn that nature had endowed him with in the form of a voice, he shouted: "Giff Villie the ball. Let Louie poosh him t'rough." Result: the winning touchdown.

It was a citizen of Louisville in this time who completed the macabre drinking chantey sung by Long John Silver in *Treasure Island* that Robert Louis Stevenson quoted for only four lines. This citizen, Young E. Allison, was the editor of a sectarian business publication, the *Insurance Field*, almost the last office where one would expect to find a poet of this genre. He was a quiet man of middle height, from whose carefully expressionless face would constantly emerge some of the wittiest observations on persons and matter that I ever have heard. And his prose, even when dealing with such droning topics as insurance, was a model of the clear and the laconic.

Stevenson's Long John Silver sang only these lines:

> Fifteen men on a dead man's chest —
> Yo ho ho and a bottle of rum —
> Drink and the devil had done for the rest —
> Yo ho ho and a bottle of rum.

To these Allison attached several stanzas, calling his poem "Derelict." This prompted James Whitcomb Riley, a poet of great fame in his time, to write: "Fifteen men on a dead man's chest / Young E. Allison done the rest." Because, most regrettably, the full text of "Derelict" appears rarely in anthologies, it is reproduced in full in the Appendix of this book.

Erotica had not yet been supplanted in modern literature by pornographic smut, and Allison and his assistant editor, Daniel E. O'Sullivan, found amusement in producing and collecting this form in their leisure hours, adding only that pornography which is in the grand vein of Rabelais. The exhibits were bundled into an ever-thickening file known as "the C. J. Printing Company Envelope." (The Courier-Journal company owned and published the *Insurance Field*.)

The few given access by Allison and O'Sullivan to the contents of the envelope got their first knowledge that Eugene Field, nationally described as "the Chil-

dren's Poet," the creator of "Wynken and Blynken
and Nod," was gifted in the composition of verses
not exactly suitable to be read by his protégés.
Among these were such celebrated items as "The
French Crisis" and "Socrates and Alcibiades." In
these works Field's bawdy genius rose above the
subject matter like the sun above a puddle. And this,
it seems to me, marks the fundamental test of what
is pornography that even the Supreme Court of the
United States should be able to decide.

At the Tavern, a club of younger men, the company was enlivened by Cleves Kinkead. He was
short, pug-nosed, the blithest of spirits, the son of
a distinguished, dignified judge, the delight of any
group, especially when the bourbon was flowing.
Soon bored with legal practice, in which he engaged
after graduating from Centre College and law school,
Kinkead one day decided to try to become a play-
wright. To this purpose he entered Professor Baker's
famous course at Harvard and wrote the required
play. With the title *Common Clay* and Jane Cowl in
the lead, the play was destined for a long run on
Broadway and equal success in the "provinces."

On the day of Kinkead's greatest triumph — the
opening of the play at Macauley's Theatre in his
home town — he encountered on Fourth Street an
old friend and schoolmate, James Keller, the drama
critic of the *Louisville Times*. Assuming the crouch

of a boxer on defense, "All I ask from you is justice," said Kinkead to Keller. "That's what I am threatening you with," was his friend's reply.

Many boardinghouses have made their way into literature and the hearts of humble patrons who became renowned. But at least three generations of theater folk, a goodly number of whom were later famous, were devoted to the Louisville institution run by Mother Savage. It was immaculately appointed; the food was superior; the rules of conduct were strict and enforced — though now and then she overlooked an infraction if she believed that "true love" was the cause; and Mother Savage extended indefinite credit to any actor or actress of good behavior who had fallen on hard times, even though gambling or a reckless buying spree was the cause.

Among the regular patrons of the small boardinghouse — it had few rooms to let — were the advance men, press agents and company managers and stars of the burlesque shows which were performed at the Buckingham Theatre. On the occasions when I was honored with an invitation to be Mother Savage's guest, the conduct of the burlesque queen in residence was almost painfully decorous. And it was well known that even the sound of a stealthy footfall in the night, in traverse from one bedroom to another, would fall like thunder on her ears and the likely

consequence would be exclusion from the house forever. In his memoirs, *Max Gordon Presents*, the famous Broadway producer attests in detail to these
and other facts of life under the Victorian eye of
Mother Savage:

Of all the places [lodgings on the road], the one I
liked best was Mother Savage's in Louisville, Kentucky.
There were four theaters in Louisville when I began
making the rounds, and Mother Savage ran a busy
place. She preferred show-people and show-people loved
her. She was kind and understanding. An actor down
on his luck knew that Mother Savage would listen and
carry a tab. She knew what a temptation the nearby
Churchill Downs races were. She knew that the police
ignored some of the local crap and poker games, and
consequently an actor could have a run of bad luck at
either. Her hostel was generally filled to capacity. But if
one of her regular customers arrived and she did not
have a room, she would find him one somewhere else,
insisting always that it be as clean and respectable as
those in her own house.

Mother Savage was no prude. She knew the ways of
the world. She permitted no shenanigans in her rooms,
but she was not averse to telling a couple where such
places could be found if she felt they were old enough
to know what they were doing. She kept many a lone-
some kid from getting into trouble. Once in a great
while, if she liked someone very much, she could look
the other way, as long as outward respectability was

maintained. I knew one young reporter, now a man of great fame in journalism, who happened to be a favorite of Mother Savage's. When a girl would invite him up to her room for a while, Mother Savage would make believe she knew nothing about it. Marc Connelly, who wrote *The Green Pastures* among other successful plays, knew Mother Savage, too. His favorite story, as well as mine in the years after, was of the time she refused to evict the owner of Magnus the Great, a brilliant performing goat. When a boarder (in the next room) complained of the smell, she told him to open his window.

"What?" he cried. "And lose my pigeons?" *

Mother Savage was a small woman, prim in manner, fair of complexion, economical and literate of speech. She was never without her badge of office — an apron. No ministering angel she, being "a creature not too bright or good / For human nature's daily food." But the wayfarer (though on a selective basis) could count on her for shelter. And this must be some of the business of heaven.

The proprietors of the "Buck," as the burlesque theater was affectionately known in Louisville, and from which much of Mother Savage's patronage was derived, were two brothers who most certainly belong in the category of the town's large crop of un-

* Max Gordon with Lewis Funke, *Max Gordon Presents*, (New York: Bernard Geis Associates, 1963), pp. 65–66.

usual characters. They were John and James Whal-
len, and since each had received commissions as
"Colonel" on the staff of a Kentucky Governor, they
were uniformly addressed as "Colonel John" and
"Colonel Jim." For many years the brothers were
very important cogs in the city's political structure,
affiliating generally with the Democratic party wing
opposed to the Haldeman faction.

Many were the campaign strategies evolved in
their offices in the theater building, and sometimes
it was there that compromises were reached between
the rival factions. In these meetings it was customary
that the Louisville police be represented, for, always
deep in politics, the police had to know the nominating
and electing game plan concerned so that they could
execute their assignment to put it in operation. This
often required documentary knowledge of the pecca-
dilloes and worse of aspiring politicians, especially of
those who were Republicans. And this knowledge
was much more powerful than their nightsticks.

Both Colonel John and Colonel Jim were spoken
of as "fine dressers": that is, they were always clad in
expensive frock-coated suits with matching waist-
coats; their watchchains were large hunks of solid
gold; their hands were adorned with diamond rings;
their costly boots shone like mirrors. Colonel John,
the older and portly, favored dark fabrics and black
fedoras; Colonel Jim's taste in clothing ran to fawn-

colored suits and fedoras of the same hue. Each was blessed with the mellifluous tone of the Irish voice, and their accent was a fetching combination of brogue and Southern drawl.

Their principal political lieutenant was Michael (Mickey) Brennan, as gifted in his calling as any machine politician anywhere. He had an assistant known to everyone as "Miss Lennie" McLaughlin, and what in later years Mrs. Moscowitz was to Governor Alfred E. Smith of New York — an indispensable, brilliant and fiercely loyal brain-trust — Miss Lennie was to Mickey Brennan.

The pair was especially gifted with a sense of what the protocol should be when a peace council between the rival factions was indicated. Miss Lennie would either say, "The General [Haldeman] should go to the Buck this time," or "Colonel John and Jim should visit the C. J. [Courier-Journal] office." When the General or the Colonels refused to make the gesture, that was tantamount to a declaration of war.

There was a roughhouse Democratic political organization, the Mose Green Club, to which it was prudent for all factions to belong because, though composed of constantly warring factions, membership was regarded as an implicit pledge to support the party ticket when the battle over selections was done. There was no "Mose Green," but the origin of the name was attributed to a long-dead Democrat of Swabian nativity who was credited with asserting the high principle that he would support that candidate who had "de mos' green [money]." The Club held an annual ball which all aspiring Democrats made it a point to attend, and the police to ignore the strong tendency of the revelers to break a number of public ordinances.

This was a time when the nation was rebuilding and setting the foundations for the economic explosion of the twentieth century, and Louisville contributed its share of builders, financial eccentrics and speculators. In Milton H. Smith, president of the Louisville & Nashville Railroad, our town boasted the presence of one of the Empire Builders. Along with James J. Hill, E. H. Harriman, Marvin Hughitt, Samuel Spencer, Collis Huntington, William H. Crocker and Mark Hopkins, he helped to link by rail the ocean coasts, and Canada with the Gulf of Mexico. One of the best-known things about Smith was that he made himself inaccessible to the press, for which he felt deep distrust. To sustain his attitude he kept a close watch of what was printed, and whenever he found a basis to challenge the credibility of the press he did so with poker-faced glee.

In the long running battle between Smith and Watterson, growing out of the ruthless methods employed by the L&N to prevent the election of William Goebel, the Democratic nominee for Governor in 1899, the railroad president once mastered the famous editor. For every hostile editorial in the *Courier-Journal*, Smith had responded so devastatingly as to fact that Watterson finally put an end to the exchange with this editorial: "To Milton H. Smith: You done outtalked me. H.W."

Professionally a leper though I was, I grew through mutual connections to know Smith and win his friendship. He would, however, never allow me to quote him in the paper, although his salty and perceptive comment would have enriched the contemporary scene. But when his eightieth birthday approached, and he had declined to allow me to publish even an up-to-date photograph of himself, I devised a trap.

I made it a point to encounter him in Central Park (a recreation area with no real claim to its pretentious name) for a few mornings in succession while he was proudly wheeling his grandson in a pram. On the third day I produced a photographer, to whom Smith raised his stick until I explained that I was sure he would like a picture of the baby. He amiably consented; I sent him several copies as promised; but the morning after the taking, the beguiling photograph of grandfather wheeling grandson appeared on the first page of the *Courier-Journal*. He forgave me, and even carried the print around in his wallet because, but only because, he said, "it was a good likeness of the baby."

In the course of his feud with the press he once, having read what purported to be his true biography in the *Herald*, wrote this to the newspaper: "The only truthful statement in the article is that my name is, yours truly, Milton H. Smith." And in the course of the great rivalry of the L&N and the Southern Railroad, Smith suggested to Spencer that they divide, as the Spanish conquistadores divided the lands they stole, the railroad business in the South. "You be Pizarro, and I Cortez," he wrote. This got into the press; Smith of course was attacked as an especially callous capitalist pirate; and he was greatly amused.

So devoted was Smith to his immediate task of building an industrial "New" South that he restricted his travel to the L&N lines and begrudged every minute away from his family and his desk. An example was his only trip abroad. The J. P. Morgan–Henry Walters interests, chief financiers of the railroad, insisted that he attend a meeting at the Bank of England of British bankers who were heavy investors in the L&N. Smith took the train to New York, embarked at that port for Liverpool, proceeded to London by rail, attended the meeting, instantly returned to Liverpool and sailed back on the ship which had brought him across the Atlantic. If he even noticed any of the historic glories of London it was only during his drives in a hansom cab from the railway station to Threadneedle Street and back.

In Smith's last years his favorite recreation was to go out to the Louisville Country Club and, sitting under a favorite tree at the edge of one of the fairways, watch the golfers at their rounds. Several always stopped to pass the time of day with him, though occasionally earning shouted protests from oncoming players who knew not Caesar. When the day came that Smith was missing from his bower, a very special Louisville landmark was gone forever.

Our prime eccentric citizen was "Cap'n" Norton. Nobody knew whence the military title, and he was not related to the other Norton family whose wealth and breeding were as outstanding as the beauty of their four daughters and their estate on the environs of Cherokee Park. But of all the "characters" in the town none was more unusual than the "Cap'n." His wealth vied in repute with his eccentricity. Once at an auction he had inexplicably bought several thousand camp chairs. He solved the question of what to do with them by building the Louisville Auditorium, explaining this was the only solution he could think of. One night the auditorium took fire and "Cap'n" Norton was summoned to the scene. He refused, and, remarking that the matter in hand was to put out the fire and "this was the job of Ed Hughes," chief of the Fire Department, went back to bed.

On a certain day each week he would don a policeman's uniform and sit on the curb at Fourth and Walnut Streets with his feet in the gutter. There beggars and persons with private troubles of all kinds, notified that Cap'n Norton would give them a hearing, assembled in large numbers. When asked why the uniform, he asked in turn whether it wasn't true that one of the best-known adages was "Tell your troubles to a policeman."

Those in Louisville who were hardest hit by the Depression of the Nineteen Thirties were those bankers and others who, years before, had begun to entrust their honor and their fortunes to a reputed financial wizard, James B. Brown. He, who had come to town from the rural county of Anderson with little more than the clothes on his back, shattered all the barriers to financial leadership that for generations had been manned by the families with old money. With a shrewdness and daring, unexampled in the history of the town, and a cynical awareness of the greed which moves men to abandon their principles, he eventually gained control of the sacrosanct Bank of Kentucky, bossed the aristocratic directors as if they were in boot camp and he a Marine drill sergeant, bought, merged (and wrecked) the *Herald* and the *Evening Post*, and thrust a controlling finger into a number of national corporations and local politics.

Soon after the entrance of the United States into the First World War he was appointed by President Wilson to membership of the Capital Issues Committee, by Secretary of the Treasury McAdoo as state director for War Savings; and, in the Harding and Coolidge Administrations, Brown was chairman of the War Finance Committee for Kentucky, Indiana, Ohio and Tennessee.

But at last he fell victim, like so many other financial adventurers in 1929, et seq., to his soaring ambition and daring. The historic Bank of Kentucky was forced to close and seal its vaults. Under the harsh penalty of double indemnity, the Bank's directors suffered losses which were crippling even to men of their wealth. And by the time of his death in 1940, Jim Brown, the great entrepreneur who had made the rich richer and himself the richest of all, reckoned in pennies the paper millions of a few years before.

In the first decade of this century, the period of these recollections, Brown was beginning to rise in the banking circles of Louisville and in the Democratic political faction led by the two Whallens. In the low political standards of that place and time he found no conflict in being simultaneously head of the liquor licensing board and part owner of a brewery.

Slender in those days, of medium height, he walked with a slight stoop and, though his manner was genial, there was also a wariness in this geniality that made me think of a cat ready to purr or claw as developments might determine. But I did not then envisage the future which was awaiting him: arcane financial coups ending in resounding disaster for Jim Brown and those who trusted him to make them richer than they were by means they elected not to know too much about.

The first of his coups grew out of the 1911 Supreme Court decision requiring the dissolving of the Standard Oil Company into separate state corporations. Brown invested in the many small oil companies which were operating in Kentucky, acquired in a large block of the stock of the new Standard Oil Company of Kentucky which was formed in part of these small units, and was a millionaire at thirty.

Fame did not attract Jim Brown, one very sensible reason being that the less he was in the public eye, the greater was the latitude in which he could advance his soaring design to be a power in the national money market. He gave his nights as well as his days to the intricate financial legerdemain in which he was engaged, and the staid staff of the sedate Bank of Kentucky clucked in bewilderment over a president whose business day began at noon, who was seldom in his official quarters, and whose desk lights were burning in the small hours. Nor could they become accustomed to a chief who, with his wife, shunned the public occasions where previous heads of the historic bank were the principal figures.

The heights to which he had ascended with patient determination were so dazzling that the precipitancy of his fall was a shock from which the banking community of the city, and the Democratic faction he masterminded, were slow to recover.

The third (or fourth) generation families which, in the first decade of this century, were the core of Louisville "society" kept their doors very firmly barred against ambitious people with "new money," however personable and achieving. The owner-publishers of the newspapers, except the *Herald*, happened to possess family backgrounds acceptable to the social arbiters. But in general those on the lower levels of the press were outsiders, as in the United Kingdom to this day, though London press lords with humble beginnings — such as Beaver-brook, Harmsworth and Thomson — long ago broke through the barriers of Belgravia and Carlton House Terrace.

The time was yet distant in Louisville when the sons of the old families entered journalism and college-bred newspapermen became the rule instead of the exception. So it was very rare that a Louisville reporter was invited to the homes of the social élite, was asked to join their clubs — the ancient Pendennis, the Tavern, the Louisville Country and the River Valley (which he couldn't have afforded anyhow) — or to attend at the Galt House the Bachelors and Benedicts dance for debutantes, the trans-Allegheny counterpart of the ancestral Philadelphia Assembly.

But in Louisville, as in New York, Charleston and Richmond, even a newspaper reporter could be admitted to these charmed circles if by chance he met the favoring eye of one of the females, dowagers in particular, who control the party lists in the United States, or was introduced by a friend who "belonged."

It was by this latter route that I met a girl to whose charms I succumbed — the channel being the *Herald* cartoonist, Fontaine Fox. I had formed with him the close friendship described previously in these pages, and also he was a Kentuckian to the manor born. On a certain holiday, having discovered that I was preparing to spend it alone as usual, Fox suggested that he take me to call on a lady who, he assured me, was as attractive as she was beautiful. It did not take me long to realize that Fox's gesture was one of enormous magnanimity, for it developed he was among the most ardent of this lady's many suitors.

She was Penelope Robinson, a member of one of Louisville's most distinguished clans, and even on first acquaintance I found that her charms exceeded Fox's description. The result was that, with Fox's volunteered encouragement, I spent as much time with her as her inclination and my working regimen allowed, and on my side, the attachment grew. We used to go horseback riding in bright mornings in the Silver Hills, in the region of New Albany, Indiana, across the Ohio, where one of her married sisters lived (once I had the thrill that comes with a mixture of love and self-esteem when she fell off her horse and I sprang from mine to the rescue). And Fox having gallantly assured me he was getting nowhere with his suit and the field was open, I occupied it to the extent that was permitted to me.

"Nelly" Robinson, as she was known, was gifted with a sweetness which enhanced her gay spirit and blonde, blue-eyed beauty. I soon transferred to her my adoration for another "Nelly," one of the loveliest girls I have ever known: witness the fact that when, years later, I saw in a Dublin gallery the Sir Joshua

Reynolds portrait of a "Miss Nelly O'Brien," I also saw in this black-haired, violet-eyed descendant of the Kings of all Ireland a remarkable resemblance to the Chicago girl by the same name to whom I had been untrue.

It was in the period when I was finishing at Lewis Institute in Chicago the college education begun at Princeton that I met this twentieth-century Nelly O'Brien. Her family were devoutly Catholic, and in the hope to win their favor for even our closely supervised relationship I accompanied her to church; and, in the proper season, followed reverently and lovingly in her wake as she prayed at the Stations of the Cross.

When I returned to Kentucky our exchanges of letters began to dwindle, as they will — save in Victorian novels. I am sure her family was pleased with this because, in thinking her too good for me, they were indubitably right as proved by the easy transition of my heart to Penelope Robinson.

But one day a summons to Panama came to Penelope from another sister who was married to an officer in the United States Marine Corps on duty in the Canal Zone. We parted, with hope on my part and some encouragement on hers, that my romantic feelings might in time be reciprocated. But a couple of months later fell the "dear John" blow. Nelly Robin-

son had engaged herself to marry a certain Major
Kinkead. Once again the Marines had the situation
well in hand.

Fate marked her for an early death, but her bright
memory has abided to this day.

Bereft of an attachment which had grown very
dear, therefore not quite fancy free — for my
wounded heart took a week or so to mend — I was
at least footloose on the town again. To be an extra
man has its advantages, since hostesses everywhere
are more intent on filling unexpectedly vacant dinner
seats with bodies than with the social talents of those
who occupy them. By now I had acquired a wide circle of agreeable female acquaintances; and Louisville
is typical of Kentucky as a whole in producing a remarkable number of beauties. Among them I still
vividly recall Miss Elizabeth Sherley, whom it was
a delight merely to look upon. She first married
Thomas Shevlin, the Yale football paladin, and, after
his death, Dr. Marshall Russell of New York City.
Whereby hangs a tale.

In the mid–Nineteen Twenties Mrs. Russell asked
me to take her son, Thomas Shevlin, Jr., aged eleven,
to the annual football game between Princeton and
Yale, this time held in New Haven. On the train
from New York, after Tommy recovered from the information that he would have to sit with me and

other Nassovians on the Princeton side, his appetite took over. With the stake his mother and I had supplied him, he bought what seemed to be bushels of peanuts and popcorn, plus many soft drinks, and all the celluloid bulldogs and "Y" banners he could find, festooning his person with these tokens of his filial loyalty.

This chanced to be the game in which a Mr. Jake Slagle emerged from the Princeton backfield to run almost the entire length of the oval for a winning touchdown. A disconsolate Tommy boarded the return train, but, his appetite appearing to have been unimpaired by sorrow, he resumed his consumption of comestibles to the point where, fearing he might burst, I took him onto the platform for air.

There we encountered a group of exultant Princetonians who, noting his assemblage of "Y's" and bulldogs, offered to present the boy with one toy tiger and one "P" banner in exchange. Drawing himself to his full height of five feet or so, Tommy said haughtily: "I don't think you know who I am. I am Thomas Shevlin, Jr." Whereupon, asking nothing in exchange, they wrapped all their Princeton symbols in a white cloth, denoting surrender, and with a dignity beyond his years he accepted them.

Not until I went to Denver, in the summer of 1908, on loan from the *Herald* to the *Cincinnati Enquirer* as a reporter of the Democratic National Convention did I fall in love again. But this time the event was to have a momentous effect on my professional and personal future.

CHAPTER FIFTEEN

N IGHT DUTY at the AP Bureau — eight P.M. until four A.M. and sometimes later — deprived me of a normal social life, of course: my routine was to go to bed with the dawn and awaken with the first descent of dusk. But soon I became used to living on the schedule of the average owl, and only once did I, with W. Shakespeare (Sonnet XXX) "mourn the expense of many a vanished sight." This was a dinner-dance for a debutante, and its importance to me arose from the following circumstances:

As previously noted, while still on the *Herald* I was chosen by John D. Wakefield, the Kentucky correspondent of the *Cincinnati Enquirer*, to serve as his legman at the two national political conventions in the summer of 1908. The Democrats assembled at Denver, and there for the first time I met General W. B. Haldeman, editor of the *Louisville Times*, part owner of the *Courier-Journal* and *Times*, and his family. It consisted of his wife and two daughters, the younger of whom, Elizabeth, was known as "Miss Lizzie," as her mother was before her.

Miss Lizzie was in every respect adorable. Her face had the inner radiance that lends special beauty to a woman: among others I have known who possess it — age cannot dim it — is Alice Roosevelt Longworth. This Haldeman daughter was also the most graceful of creatures; nature had endowed her with the gift of mirth, but also awareness that life is a serious business; and her possession of a voice like Cordelia's and the most cultivated of Southern accents charmed the ear. Of the romance that quickly invested our relationship I fondly remember, after more than sixty years, that in company she would indicate a kiss for me by framing her lips to form the word "perfect," a secret arrangement of her own devising.

After we both returned to Louisville, we saw as much of each other as my nocturnal duty, her family and the preparations for her forthcoming debut would allow. Soon after that occasion — to attend which I was denied by a deluge of late news — she went abroad with her family (this was toward the end of summer in 1908), ringed by and secretly engaged to me, for consummation at a date uncertain.

We wrote constantly to each other as her tour proceeded. If Jove was laughing at these lovers' vows, as he is reputed to do, we did not recognize him as a god, anyhow. And though a friend of mine, Arthur Hopkins, cynically predicted that as her absence lengthened, postcards would supplant letters and then even postcards would cease, the fact continued to refute him. I remember he said: "The last you will hear will be a postcard, dated Moscow, informing you that there they call buggies droshkies." He was wrong.

But the correspondence did end, with the romance, and tragically. In September a cablegram from General Haldeman advised me that Miss Lizzie had died in Paris of peritonitis, following an operation required by a suddenly burst appendix. Days later her last letter was delivered to me. Interrupting a sentence in which she was describing some pleasant occasion, were these words in a faltering script: "I have just felt a most excruciat . . ." And a slashing downstroke showed all too clearly the fall of the pen from her hand.

My wound was long in healing, and the pain was intensified rather than assuaged by elegiac verses I wrote under the title "Memorabilia" and collected in a book I gave her mother. So it was a very sad and lonely young man, engaged in all-night duty in the Associated Press Bureau, to whom a telephone call came late in the year 1909 that changed my life entirely and opened a future I never had envisaged.

The telephone call was from Miss Lizzie's father: "How would you like to go to Washington as the correspondent of the *Louisville Times*?" Would I like to knock at the gate of the heaven of an aspiring political reporter? Almost before General Haldeman completed the question he had my eager acceptance. Thus it was that, a few months after the inauguration of President William H. Taft in the midst of a blizzard that broke all the climatic records of the capital city in March, I got off the train in Washington, proceeded to the St. James Hotel (two dollars a day for lodging), unpacked my one suitcase, paid my respects to, and got a frosty reception from, the aged correspondent of the prestigious sister paper of the *Times* — the *Courier-Journal* — went to the National Press Club, and got happily drunk.

Thus began for me the new and awesome phase of national journalism that was to post me twice in Washington: for the Haldeman papers (1910–1915) and for the *New York Times* (1932–1966).

APPENDIX

DERELICT

"Fifteen men on the Dead Man's Chest —
  Yo-ho-ho and a bottle of rum!
Drink and the devil had done for the rest —
  Yo-ho-ho and a bottle of rum!"
The mate was fixed by the bos'n's pike,
The bos'n brained with a marlinspike,
And Cookey's throat was marked belike
        It had been gripped
          By fingers ten;
        And there they lay,
          All good dead men,
Like break-o'-day in a boozing-ken —
  Yo-ho-ho and a bottle of rum!

Fifteen men of a whole ship's list —
  Yo-ho-ho and a bottle of rum!
Dead and bedamned and the rest gone whist! —
  Yo-ho-ho and a bottle of rum!
The skipper lay with his nob in gore
Where the scullion's ax his cheek had shore —
And the scullion he was stabbed times four.
        And there they lay,
          And the soggy skies

Dripped all day long
In upstaring eyes —
At murk sunset and at foul sunrise —
Yo-ho-ho and a bottle of rum!

Fifteen men of 'em stiff and stark —
Yo-ho-ho and a bottle of rum!
Ten of the crew had the Murder mark —
Yo-ho-ho and a bottle of rum!
'Twas a cutlass swipe, or an ounce of lead,
Or a yawing hole in a battered head —
And the scuppers glut with a rotting red.
And there they lay —
Aye, damn my eyes! —
All lookouts clapped
On Paradise —
All souls bound just contrariwise —
Yo-ho-ho and a bottle of rum!

Fifteen men of 'em good and true —
Yo-ho-ho and a bottle of rum!
Every man jack could ha' sailed with Old Pew —
Yo-ho-ho and a bottle of rum!
There was chest on chest full of Spanish gold,
With a ton of plate in the middle hold,
And the cabins riot of stuff untold.
And they lay there,
That had took the plum,
With sightless glare
And their eyes struck dumb,
While we shared all by the rule of thumb —

Yo-ho-ho and a bottle of rum!
More was seen through the sternlight screen —
Yo-ho-ho and a bottle of rum!
Chartings ondoubt where a woman had been!—
Yo-ho-ho and a bottle of rum!
A flimsy shift on a bunker cot,
With a thin dirk slot through the bosom spot
And the lace stiff-dry in a purplish blot.
Or was she wench . . .
Or some shuddering maid . . . ?
That dared the knife —
And that took the blade!
By God! she was stuff for a plucky jade —
Yo-ho-ho and a bottle of rum!

Fifteen men on the Dead Man's Chest —
Yo-ho-ho and a bottle of rum!
Drink and the devil had done for the rest —
Yo-ho-ho and a bottle of rum!
We wrapped 'em all in a mains'l tight,
With twice ten turns of a hawser's bight,
And we heaved 'em over and out of sight —
With a yo-heave-ho!
And a fare-you-well!
And a sullen plunge
In the sullen swell,
Ten fathoms deep on the road to hell!
Yo-ho-ho and a bottle of rum!

— YOUNG E. ALLISON